MORE
LIFE
MOMENTS
WITH
JOY

God's blessing!
Joy

JOY BACH

WORDS BY DESIGN

More Life Moments With Joy
Published by Words by Design
www.joy-lifemoments.blogspot.com

© 2019 Joy Bach

ISBN: 978-0-9994956-2-9 (paperback)

Cover Design: Matt McClay, McClay Design
Layout & Editing: Deborah Porter, Breath of Fresh Air Press

My Heartfelt Thanks

In the 1970s, with my previous life behind me and a brand new life beginning in Idaho, Pastor Clarence Kinzler became my confidant as I explored a new way of living. One day, he handed me a blank journal and said, "You need to start writing down what's going on in your life. Some day you're going to write a book."

Fast forward forty years and another pastor spoke into my life. I had begun writing a blog and Pastor Larry Regenfuss said, "You need to put your blogs into a book. Preachers could use your ideas in their sermons."

I dedicate this book to those two men and to the individuals who have encouraged me as I've traveled this writing journey. Without your love and support, I might never have had the courage to climb out of my secure little box. It was scary to open myself up to the world. There aren't enough words to express how much you are appreciated.

And last, but certainly not least, I am so grateful to the Holy Spirit who sat beside me as my fingers worked the keyboard. May His words speak to you.

Introduction

I HAVE KNOWN JOY BACH, the author of *More Life Moments With Joy,* all my life. She is my Mom.

If you read her first book, *Life Moments with Joy*, then you know how she looks at and responds to the world around her. If you haven't read her previous book, then you are in for a treat!

Joy's perception of daily life is deep and thoughtful. She takes the time to reflect and learn from the lessons presented by her experiences. Something as ordinary as taking her dog Charlie to obedience class (where he learned to "leave it") becomes a powerful life lesson.

Some of the stories in these pages relate family events that I remember well. I have now enjoyed these memories through a different perspective and a greater appreciation for her wisdom and experience. Joy reminds us that there is something to be learned in every Life Moment. We can take a bit of time to look for meaning in so many moments of our day. The examples in this book are a template for a new way of looking at life. Some are funny, and some are touching. All provide us with the chance to deepen our understanding of who we are and how we choose to relate to the world and those around us.

Joy Bach has faced many challenges in her life. Through it all, her faith and strength have sustained her. Once again, she has shared her Life Moments to help us all appreciate our personal journeys. She has been successful in many areas of her life, including a lifelong dream to publish a book. Now we have the gift of a second volume of Life Moments.

I am so proud of her!

Tammi Reed
June 19, 2019

Contents

A Voice From the Past

THE TREE IN OUR backyard begged to be climbed. The outstretched branches were perfect for sitting, but I wasn't supposed to be in that tree. I was a little girl in a dress. My place was quietly sitting in a corner.

Growing up, my playmates were my nieces and nephews. Some of them lived in the same town; others came to visit on weekends. Two nieces and one nephew were very close in age.

It was the nephew, Allen, who did me in. We climbed the tree, and wouldn't you know it, we planted our feet in the same crook, at the same time, and got stuck. The consequence eludes my memory, but the tree climbing was a highlight of my four-year old life.

Perfect trees, designed for climbing and sitting, still catch my attention.

Fast forward to early last Tuesday. I had been having computer issues and was unable to post my blog. So I sent a little blurb to my distribution lists that I was having computer trouble and would return when I could.

Tuesday morning at work, I received a phone call. It was Allen—truly a voice from the past. I'm not sure how many years it's been since I saw him. Twenty? Thirty? But guess what? He works on computers. That evening, it was a delight to get caught up, and the tree-climbing incident was recalled.

Allen helped me fix my computer, walking me slowly and carefully through the steps.

As I thought about this event, I wondered how many people used to have a relationship with Jesus—walking with Him, talking with Him, maybe even climbing a tree to view His world. And then the years pass, distance happens, and we lose touch.

Now we have issues.

But Jesus is a Master of all trades. No matter what is broken, He cares and wants us to reach out to Him.

Don't let Him be just a Voice from the past.

Hebrews 3:15 NLT
"Remember what it says: 'Today when you hear his voice, don't harden your hearts as Israel did when they rebelled.'"

God's Agenda

I CAREFULLY EXPLAINED TO God that I was never getting married again. Then I softened that declaration a little by saying, "If you want me to get married again, you are going to have to plant him right in front of me."

Think God can't do that?

Friends had been inviting me to attend their church. With the breakup of my marriage, I had been on a mission to become a healthy, real person, not a robot obeying anyone in authority. As part of that mission, I was in search of a church that was real too. So I agreed to visit their church. That's how it all began.

The Sunday I visited just happened to be the Sunday the new leaders for the next year were introduced. I listened as they spoke of classes for small children, teenagers, young marrieds, etc. When they were all through, no mention had been made of a class for singles, of which I was one. At the church I currently attended, I had been instrumental in getting such a group started.

As I pondered the lack of a singles' group in this church, I knew without a doubt God was telling me to go to the pastor and offer my services to help him start one. My heart pounded as I argued with God. "I can't do that. I don't even know the man. This isn't my church. I'm not strong enough yet to do that."

My heart pounded on. But God won.

After the service, I forced myself to walk to the front of the church and extend my help to the pastor. When I commented there had been no group for singles mentioned in his introductions, he whipped out a little notepad and said, "No, we don't have one yet, but we're working on it. If you give me your name and address, I'll let you know when we have one up and running."

"No, I'm here to offer my services to help you get one going."

"Good. You're number two."

Number two? I asked the pastor to explain.

"I asked God to send me three people to help get a singles' group started. You're the second person to volunteer."

Guess who the first person was? You got it. The man I eventually married.

Romans 8:28 NIV
"And we know that in all things God works for the good of those who love him, who have been called according to his purpose."

Worth Fighting Over

BACK IN THE LATE 1960s, I happened to live in the Washington DC area. George Washington's birthday on February 22 was a big deal with lots of gigantic sales.

My sister-in-law, who lived in the same area, was a shopper—something I had never been. She decided to show me how it was done. Since we both sewed, she chose a fabric store as the site where my shopping lesson would occur. Lace trim was on sale for 22 cents a yard. So we entered the fray.

I had never witnessed anything like it. She waded right in, elbows flying, along with some shoving. Not nice words from many mouths assaulted my ears.

"Come on. You'll never get anything standing back there."

I refused. No lace on earth was worth that cat fight.

She did share her spoils and I have remnants of that lace trim today.

My memory of that day is still very clear, even all these years later, and I am left to wonder what I believe is important enough to fight over like that?

Ultimately, very few things.

Saving the life of a loved one is high on my priority list—husband and children—and I would try to defend the defenseless. But there is one situation that calls for my undivided allegiance, and that is my stand for Christ. I've never been asked to choose between Him and death, but in some countries that is a regular occurrence. With a gun to my head, would I still fight for my loyalty to Christ?

It's a choice we may be demanded to make some day.

Revelations 6:9 NASB

"When the Lamb broke the fifth seal, I saw underneath the altar the souls of those who had been slain because of the word of God, and because of the testimony which they had maintained."

Words in a Book

WHEN I WAS STRUGGLING through the de-programming of my religious training, I stumbled across a book called *Your Erroneous Zones* by Dr. Wayne Dyer. Upon completion of the book, I immediately read it again, and again. The thoughts in that book were totally contrary to the beliefs I had been taught.

Thanks to that book, I learned I did not have to live daily with worry and guilt. I wore the original book out, but have a copy on my bookshelf today. The words in that book were an inspiration that helped change my life.

In a book entitled *Beyond Ourselves,* Catherine Marshall wrote a chapter on *The Prayer of Relinquishment.* I had been taught to pray telling God what I desired, such as healing, and then He was obligated to do what I asked. However, when you pray the prayer of relinquishment, you are, in essence, telling God you are willing to let Him decide what is best for you. *Beyond Ourselves* was another life changing concept. Again, the inspiration I received from those words has helped me many times in my life. I have a copy of that book on my shelf, too.

Then there was one book title that caught my eye—*I Ain't Well—but I Sure am Better* by Jess Lair, Ph.D. It was inspiring to discover that each day I could be better than I was the day before. I still have a copy of that book on my shelf.

Rosalind Rinker wrote a book called *Prayer: Conversing with God*—a truly controversial topic. It described prayer as a conversation with God, and my fear of the heresy within its pages almost prevented me from progressing through the book. I knew how to pray in King James language and how to pray to impress others. The concept of simply talking to God seemed disrespectful, but the insight I received from the words in that book changed my prayer life forever. It, too, has a special place on my bookshelf.

These books, and many others, were written in the 60s and 70s, and yet they are still so very special to me today. How satisfying it must be for authors to realize that their words in a book have helped trigger personal growth in someone's life.

Of course, there is also the Bible, written long before 1960. Even though many centuries have passed, I continually discover something new and life changing from the words in that Book. I have several versions on my shelf.

As a writer, I pray that some day, somewhere, some how, I will write words that inspire someone to change their life for the better. Words they will carry with them.

Jeremiah 30:2 MSG

"Write everything I tell you in a book"

A Good Night's Sleep

It's bedtime and I climb into bed. I exchange a few goodnight words with the love of my life, and I go to sleep. Isn't that what going to bed is for? Night after night, I sleep soundly and awaken when the alarm goes off.

Not so this night.

I try to stifle the cough I feel building in my throat. Finally it explodes into the air.

I change positions. Still coughing.

I lay on my face. Doesn't help.

The coughing is relentless.

I slip from the bed, picking up my slippers and housecoat as I leave the room.

The clock chimes 1:15.

Moving quietly to the TV room, I use the leather stuffed chair as a bed, placing a cover over me. I cough on.

The clock chimes 1:30.

I think of my friend who lies in a hospital bed after having cranial surgery for eight hours. She's not having such a good night. And what about all those homeless people I saw in Seattle a few weeks ago. Do they ever get a good night's sleep?

And the coughing continues.

The clock chimes 1:45.

On this night, there are people in Alabama trying to sleep on the floor of a gymnasium with hundreds of other people. Their homes have been destroyed. They aren't getting a good night's sleep. And what about the brave souls who are in places like Afghanistan, fighting to help keep our world a better place? They would love to be sitting in a chair in my peaceful home.

My coughing fit seems to be over. I sneak back to bed.

The clock chimes 2:00.

My head hits the pillow and I cough. I grit my teeth and turn over. I cough again. Quickly moving through all the sleeping positions known to man, I try to find one that will stifle the coughing. It is not to be.

The clock chimes 2:15.

Once again, I sneak from the bedroom, but this time I don't head for the chair in the TV room. I'm wide-awake, so I walk to my office and turn on the light. The computer beckons me. I've got words in my head to put on paper. And so I type these words.

The clock chimes 2:30.

I would like to have a good night's sleep. But since I can't, I've talked to you.

Psalm 3:5 (NLT)

"I lay down and slept, yet I woke up in safety, for the LORD was watching over me."

A Broken Commitment

I TRIED TO CARE. I really did. Twice I pushed myself out of my cocoon of pillows and covers and walked to my desk, sat at the keyboard and stared. Guilt washed over me. I had made a commitment to myself that I would write every day. Now, I was reneging on that. No words flowed from my fingers because no words were available in my brain.

I was sick.

For over a week my world had been a blur. On three of those days I had needed to go to work. The energy I expelled in arising, sitting, showering, sitting, dressing, sitting, and then driving to my place of employment exhausted me as though I had run a marathon.

Weakling.

And the nights. Coughing so hard I literally saw flashes of light in my closed eyes. All the time wondering if my husband was getting any sleep.

In the spaces between coughing fits, I slept so hard I never knew when he showered and left for work.

My daily exercise routine was cast aside.

I know you've been there. It's no fun.

Now in the recovery stage, as my mind begins to function again (scary thought), I think of those who have no recovery phase. Those injured in Iraq who made promises to return to loved ones. They have, but for some, they will never see again, never take their children for a Sunday drive, or never have the ability to think clearly. They will live with broken commitments for the rest of their lives.

I'm grateful for being able to breathe again, to eat food that doesn't taste like cardboard, and to know I will recover. My heart goes out to those who deal with the broken promises due to shattered bodies or minds.

May they feel God's arms around them as they grasp a new way of living.

Job 2:10b (NLT)
"Should we accept only good things from the hand of God and never anything bad?"

Who Told You?

Chuck Swindoll asked a question that caused me to think, on and on. Who told you about Jesus and led you to Him?

At the age of six, my mother told me to go to the altar and receive Christ. So I went to the altar. I have no memory of it, but I always did what I was told. This was a story she repeated through the years.

The church we attended didn't really talk about Jesus. It was all about God and His anger toward us.

My teen years were filled with multiple trips to the altar, always because my mother said so. I felt no joy in those trips, just relief that she would leave me alone for a week or so. Each trip was because, in some way, I had displeased God.

No mention of Jesus and His love.

I was told to marry the preacher's son, and I did. He became a preacher, but espoused the same religion his father had delivered. He certainly did not ever talk to me about Jesus. And so I continued to live in obedience to a doctrine that expected me to live by the list of rules dictated by our church.

No mention of Jesus and His love.

Then came the day that I was lying on my back in a hospital bed. I had been there for several days, bleeding internally. The doctors were searching for the cause.

Even though I had prayed the required prayers all my life, I had never talked to God. Yet, at that moment, I had no one else to turn to, so I asked, "God, I have done all that you have required of me. I've lived by the 637 rules of conduct, so why am I here? What did I do wrong to deserve this?"

I saw no flash of light, heard no thunder, but very clearly heard, "I have no grandchildren."

That was not helpful. What, exactly, did that mean?

Since I had plenty of time to ponder in my hospital bed, my mind went to work.

My whole life had been lived under the direction of a human telling me what God wanted of me. As the days passed in hospital, I came to understand that God wanted a relationship with me. This was a totally foreign concept.

During the ten days I lay in that hospital bed, I began a relationship. No human came to my bedside, but Jesus was with me in that room. When I was discharged, I returned home a different person.

I was no longer a grandchild, but a child of God.

Who told you? Can you remember the people who pointed you in the direction of God's love?

And now I ponder my life. Who have I told about Jesus? Can anyone point to me and say that I helped them understand about His love?

Hebrews 4:2 (NIV)

"For we also have had the good news proclaimed to us ..."

Feeling Oh So Proud

THE CHANGE IN ME over the previous years was nothing less than remarkable. I had grown from an insecure, no self-esteem, robotic self to a confident person of worth. So, this journey by car from Washington to California, all by myself, was proof to me I had pretty much arrived.

That's a long trip and required stopping to eat. I pulled my car into a parking spot and entered the restaurant. No longer did I quake when I needed to eat alone in public. It felt good to know how to peruse the menu and decide for myself what I wanted to eat.

A good book to read, a good lunch to consume, and it was time to hit the road again, but I chose to use the restroom before heading back to the car. As I traversed the restaurant from the restroom to the front door, I was delighted by the number of people who smiled at me. I tried to make eye contact with everyone.

Back at the car, I opened the driver's door and lifted my foot to climb in. That's when I noticed it. The end of the toilet paper roll had stuck to the bottom of my shoe. I had left a trail behind me on my way through the restaurant. No wonder they smiled.

Ever had a moment like that?

I will never have to see those people again, I thought as I drove on down the highway. But my thoughts ricocheted from embarrassment, to relief that it was over, to wondering exactly how it had happened. *Do I have gum on my shoe? I'll check later, but just get me out of here.*

Then God showed up and we had a little talk. Or rather, He talked and I listened. Did I really think I got to where I was in my growth without help? Did I not know that He had been there as I took those baby steps?

Life is a journey toward wholeness.

I no longer felt I'd arrived, but that didn't take away the change in me. I was still confident, but even though I had put some hard work into the change, the credit goes to Someone who loved me through it.

Romans 15:17 (MSG)
"Looking back over what has been accomplished and what I have observed, I must say I am most pleased—in the context of Jesus, I'd even say proud ..."

The Cycle of Life

EARLY YESTERDAY MORNING I received a text, accompanied by a picture. Thirty minutes earlier our close friends had welcomed their first grandchild into the world. A smile came easily to my lips. So I put that picture as wallpaper on my iPhone. All day, each time I used my phone, there was the picture of that precious baby.

I smiled, and I needed to smile.

As a bookkeeper, I'm in the process of gathering all the information needed to take to the accountant for tax purposes. My workday was full, and I was tired when I got home.

While relaxing on the couch, my iPhone rang. Another picture appeared on the screen. It was my brother—the younger of two brothers. We weren't very far into the conversation when I realized the reason for the call. He wanted me to be aware of our older brother's condition. He was declining rapidly.

Ending the phone call, I sat on the couch. No more smile. Tears flowed. My older brother had married and moved away when I was four, so I've not been really close to him. I have a few memories of visits with him through the years, but one memory stands out clearly in my mind.

That brother drove from Colorado to Nebraska one Saturday to sit on my front porch and teach me how to think for myself. Having been raised under religious oppression, I had been taught what to think. I lived in a cage of fear. That day, for four hours, he snipped away at those bars until he finally broke through the barrier. He drove back to Colorado, and I chose a different life path that led to the fulfilling life I have today.

And so, I grieve.

Ecclesiastes 3:1-2, 4 (NIV)
"There is a time for everything, and a season for every activity under the heavens: a time to be born and a time to die, a time to plant and a time to uproot ... a time to weep and a time to laugh, a time to mourn and a time to dance."

The Peanut Butter Jar

HAVING BEEN RAISED TO believe God was waiting around the next corner to zap me if I breathed wrong, I was filled with fear and hopelessness. When I was fifteen, my mother allowed the church to begin making arrangements for my marriage to the preacher's son. Totally aware I had no choice in the matter, I accepted that fate and married when I was barely seventeen, leaving high school and moving to another state. And then, after thirteen years, he left.

Battered, bruised, no self-confidence, and feeling hopeless, it took me two years to get the courage to decide I even had any value worth working on. As my confidence slowly grew, I joined a church choir.

Then came the weekend the choir went away for a retreat.

I was terrified but longed to be included. I had no extra money, but someone offered to pay my way. Someone else gave me a ride in their car. That's how I ended up sitting at the feet of a man whose words helped change my life.

He began to speak of having crystal glasses and china dishes in the cupboard. I couldn't relate. We had never had either. He talked of how those glasses and dishes were saved for "good," and how wasted they were, because "good" only happened once or twice a year.

His words turned to the peanut butter jar. It comes home in the grocery bag. Someone puts it in the cupboard. The kids get it out to make sandwiches. Over the days, it becomes empty. Somehow it ends up in the dishwasher. When the clean dishes are taken out of the dishwasher, the empty peanut butter jar is placed in the cupboard, with part of the label still stuck on. Someone is thirsty, reaches in the cupboard and gets the jar to use for a drink. And the cycle begins. It goes back in the dishwasher. Maybe this time it gets chipped or a little bit more of the label comes off. But it is a vital part of daily life.

While that picture was clear in our minds, he opened his Bible to Colossians 1:27b. *"This is the secret: Christ lives in you."*

He began to explain how we are all vessels. Some are like exquisite crystal, but they rarely do "good." I'm sure my eyes opened wider and wider. Those were the people I had been taught to revere and model after. Somehow, I was never quite "good" enough.

When he began to talk about the "peanut butter jar" people, tears ran down my cheeks. There I sat, with my jar chipped and labeled, and he was telling me I was a vessel—one that could be a vital part of the everyday life of the Christian.

I didn't change overnight, but I had a secret. Christ was in ME. My job was to be the vessel.

I sat a peanut butter jar on our counter at home as a constant reminder. I knew with every fiber of my being that I could be a peanut butter jar!

The vessel is not the important part. It is what we contain.

You may not be a "peanut butter jar," but I'm sure you know someone who is. They may be very quiet and distant, or rough around the edges with tattoos and piercings. Perhaps they are just angry. Maybe they have a lot of illnesses that are psychosomatic. They don't know it yet, but they can be vessels containing a secret—Christ. It is our job to let them in on that secret.

Each time I see a peanut butter jar, I am reminded of that evening long ago. I may be chipped and still have some labels stuck on me, but I am a vessel containing the incredible secret that Christ lives in me.

Colossians 1:27b (NLT)

"And this is the secret: Christ lives in you. This gives you assurance of sharing his glory."

WHYAMI

I HAVE PERSONALIZED LICENSE plates. They say WHYAMI. Yes, they do. I've been made fun of a great deal.

In my effort to get a message across to the people sitting in the lane behind me, walking past my car at the gym, or sitting at Starbucks, I wanted my plates to say something like PURPOSE or CHOICES. You are only allowed to have seven letters and those words were already taken.

One day I parked my car at Starbucks and walked toward the door. A young man I had never seen before was sitting at an outside table. As I walked by, he asked, "So, have you figured it out yet?"

It took me a moment, but what an opening. "Yes, I have."

Suddenly I was in the midst of a Divine appointment.

Another impact from having such specialized plates is that I am recognizable. Thus, I became very aware of how I was driving. I am trying to send a positive message, which just won't work if I cut someone off in traffic. And the police would certainly have no trouble identifying my car.

If you say you are a Christ-follower, then you have people reading you. Are you sending conflicting messages? You never know when you might have a Divine appointment.

Hebrews 10:36 (MSG)
"But you need to stick it out, staying with God's plan so you'll be there for the promised completion."

A Momentous Weekend

IN THE 1990s, I FELT God's tug on my heart. Most of the time when that happens, it means I will have to stretch and grow. So I said, "Not yet. I'm not ready." But have you ever noticed that tug doesn't go away? As the years passed, the tug grew stronger. If I submitted, it would mean standing in front of a group of women and sharing my story.

You don't think that sounds scary? That's nice. It terrified me.

Thus began my painful and frightening journey into public speaking. Attending Toastmasters week after week, reading and memorizing my speeches. I struggled on. After completing all the Toastmaster manuals, I knew how to organize a speech, how to talk without filler words and to omit the sound of *uh* from my talk.

That's all well and good, but I was still scared.

Years passed and I saw no women in front of me, waiting for me to open my mouth and have my story come forth. Then one weekend that all changed.

God chose a perfect group of women to be my guinea pigs. Of course, they were unaware that was their role. They exhibited such kind and gentle spirits, extending their love to me and welcoming me with open arms. As I stood before them, they allowed me to shed tears, and then gave me time to gather myself and continue. My story is such a wonderful story of God's grace that it still overwhelms me.

On the train after that first speaking opportunity, with the wheels clacking and my iPad rocking as I pecked with one finger, I thought, *I'm headed home, but I am not the same.* Had I really believed God wouldn't come through this time? Shame on me. I spent no sleepless nights, suffered no upset stomach, endured no pounding heart. I had a few notes, but didn't use them. Many people were praying for my time of speaking and their prayers held me steady.

God had worked in my life again. He's awesome.

1 Thessalonians 5:34 (NASB)
"Faithful is He who calls you, and He also will bring it to pass."

A Matter of Trust

As I walked down the hallway of our home, our newly rescued dog Charlie bounded by my side. In the laundry room, I petted, praised, and then gave him a treat.

When I reached the kitchen, I turned to see why he was making such a funny sound. He was madly pawing at the sides of his mouth, finally falling to the floor.

I ran for the laundry room, reached for his mouth and pulled it open. He just lay there, which caused a quick reaction on my part. *This is worse than I thought.*

With me holding onto his jaws, Charlie moved to a sitting position. I could see down his throat. The dog biscuit was stuck crosswise in there. Knowing that his teeth could do severe damage to my hand if he closed his mouth, I reached for the back of his throat, hooked my finger around the biscuit and pulled. It took a quick jerk to dislodge the firmly stuck biscuit.

The whole time, Charlie never made a sound or a move. He trusted me.

That caused me to think a lot about trust. It goes both ways. I had to trust that Charlie would not bite me, and he had to trust that I was helping him.

It's the same with people. Are there some people you don't trust? Can they trust you with their feelings, their faults, and their dreams?

Then there is God. For many years, I did not trust Him, and I certainly was not worthy of His trust. But now I have entrusted my life to Him.

Just as I had to grab Charlie's jaws, pry them open, and reach down his throat (which I'm sure he didn't like or enjoy), I have to trust God when I feel things aren't going the way I would like.

It's a matter of trust.

Matthew 6:34 (MSG)
"Give your entire attention to what God is doing right now, and don't get worked up about what may or may not happen tomorrow. God will help you deal with whatever hard things come up when the time comes."

That Door is Always Open

WHEN WE LEAVE THE house, we put Charlie in the backyard. When we return, he hears the garage door opener and dashes to the back door to be let in. However, when the days grew hot, he discovered a cool spot on the north side of the house. From there, he wasn't able to hear when we arrived home.

One morning, after running errands and grocery shopping, I came into the house, but Charlie did not come running to the back door. I opened it and called his name.

Still, no Charlie.

I pushed the door almost shut but did not latch it. Then I carried the groceries into the house.

Still no Charlie.

I worked around the house a little more, even going to the bedroom on the north side and calling his name. We've taught him how to push a door open, so he could come in if he wanted.

I waited.

Suddenly, there he was at the door, tail wagging. I called out, "Come on," but he just stood there with his tongue hanging out and his whole body wiggling.

That meade me think of some people I know who are standing at the door of a relationship with Jesus. The door is unlatched and ready for them to walk through. Jesus is saying, "Come on," but they stand there, being friendly, watching what's going on inside. They never take that final step of pushing the door open and walking through.

That door is always open.

Luke 14:16-20 (NLT)
"A man prepared a great feast and sent out many invitations. When the banquet was ready, he sent his servant to tell the guests, 'Come, the banquet is ready.' But they all began making excuses. One said, 'I have just bought a field and must inspect it. Please excuse me.' Another said, 'I have just bought five pairs of oxen, and I want to try them out. Please excuse me.' Another said, 'I now have a wife, so I can't come.'"

Out of the Nest

UNDER A DEADLINE TO complete my current afghan project, I took it to the backyard swing to enjoy the beautiful day while I worked. There are four bird feeders in the garden and the birds were singing. As I crocheted, I talked to God about my gratitude for His blessings.

But one robin wasn't singing. It was declaring an emergency.

Charlie froze in position with his nose stuck in an evergreen. I'd seen him do that before when he saw something, but usually it was short-lived and he would go about his business. This time, the robin was still in distress and Charlie was halfway into the tree. *Maybe these two things are connected,* I thought.

I called Charlie to leave the tree. He didn't budge.

I laid my afghan project on the swing and walked toward the tree. Charlie stayed frozen and the robin sounded desperate. Taking Charlie by the collar, I led him inside the house. Then I returned to the tree.

I knelt down and began to look for the problem. And then I spied it—a baby bird had fallen from the nest. I wanted to help, but what could I do?

I returned to the house, with Charlie at the door determined to go back outside. Putting on some gloves, I returned to the tree and crawled closer to the baby. Momma shrieked and flew around my head as I pondered my next move. Reaching for the baby caused it to flutter and leave the protection of the tree. Now it was out in the open on the rocks. Momma was still going crazy.

I moved to the other side of the tree, creeping closer. Even if I did get the baby bird, then what? I didn't see a nest.

It didn't work. The baby was still on the ground. The momma was still signaling distress. I had to leave them (and ban Charlie from the backyard).

Our relationship with God can be like that. All He wants to do is help, but we reject His advances. Instead, we turn to others—spouse, friend, pastor—for advice and guidance. For some, God is a big, scary thing that causes fear. It used to be that way for me, but not anymore.

I've fallen out of the nest, and He has gently picked me up and situated me in a place of safety. He'll do that for you too.

Psalm 91:9 (MSG)
"His huge outstretched arms protect you—under them you're perfectly safe."

Work in Progress

WHEN MY HUSBAND AND I had our home built, we didn't quite understand the wind patterns and the tunnel effect that would occur between our house and the one to the south. Sometimes our winds blow 40-50 miles per hour from the southwest. Soon we learned that those winds would cause our lawn swing and chairs on the patio to take wing and fly over the fire pit.

We talked it over and decided to wall off the south end of the patio—stucco with tile in the center. Good idea.

Plans were put in motion, tile chosen, and the design for placement of those tiles laid out on our patio floor. We took a ten-day vacation expecting the wall to be complete when we returned.

It wasn't.

Days passed.

And then a week.

And then two.

Finally, work began and, after a while, was completed.

As I had watched and waited, my thoughts turned to my personal progress in life, but the delays and stagnation in my growth were not a matter of days or even weeks. This project has taken years, and God is not through with me yet.

I can hardly wait to see the finished me!

Philippians 1:6 (NLT)
"And I am certain that God, who began the good work within you, will continue his work until it is finally finished."

A Dream Delayed

Measurements are a funny thing. They need to be correct. As a seamstress, I understand that if I measure incorrectly, the clothes will not fit. Usually the error can be fixed, but with frustrating hours of ripping out, re-cutting, and re-sewing. The same criteria are true for many other areas, such as baking a cake or building a house.

Measurements also need to be correct for constructing tables, shelves, and a cutting table for sewing.

Somehow, the measurements for my cutting table were wrong. It's a gorgeous table, built on wheels so I can move it out from the wall, and with a fold-down extension on the back. The drawers and doors are designed specifically for my stuff. But it's too long to fit in the intended spot.

Thus, the bookshelf that was to go on that wall had to be moved to another wall. That required further rearranging of the bookshelves, along with moving the existing furniture about three inches.

The Formica shelf attached to the side of the bookshelf, for my iron when I'm ironing, had to be removed.

And I'm on hold.

Delayed dreams are frustrating. Being in limbo is unsettling.

I felt so sorry for the builder, who took it very hard. But that is exactly the way life works. Rearranging a room is not the end of the world.

Who knows? Maybe the end result will be better than I planned.

Proverbs 19:21 (MSG)
"We humans keep brainstorming options and plans, but God's purpose prevails."

The Knock on the Door

THE PLANS HAD BEEN LAID. Romantic music at the ready. Scented candles lit. Dinner on the table. John was ready. The big question would be asked tonight. I saw it coming.

And I also knew something that he, apparently, didn't know.

He had planned this evening on Halloween.

We sat on the couch, wine glasses in hand, and it was about time for that question.

There was a knock on the door.

"Who in the world could that be?"

The sweet little sound of "Trick or treat," wafted my way.

The look on John's face was priceless. "Is this Halloween?"

So much for plans. His fell apart.

But life is like that. We plan our career, marry our beloved, build a wonderful home, and we think we are set. Then comes the knock on the door. It's not a sweet little voice. It comes in the form of layoffs, divorce, foreclosure, sickness or death.

So much for our plans. They can fall apart.

But that's where God comes in. Nothing surprises Him and He can handle whatever the situation.

As a Christ-follower, the peace remains no matter what the knock on the door brings.

God's plans never fall apart.

Micah 4:12 (NLT)
"But they do not know the Lord's thoughts or understand his plan."

Turtle Religion

I REMEMBER THE DAY John and I took a walk in the drizzle, which turned to rain. We had dressed for the occasion, in our waterproof jackets with hoods. Unfortunately, my head wasn't big enough (surprise) for the hood. No matter how I fixed the strings and Velcro, the bill on the hood kept sliding down, making a roof over my glasses. I couldn't see very well. In fact, I could only see straight ahead.

Crossing streets was an issue. Like a turtle, I poked my head out (by pulling my hood back) to check for cars.

I could hear John beside me, but that was the only way I could tell my husband was walking with me. As for communication, that was muffled by the hood.

As I walked, I thought about some churches I've been in. That is exactly what they require of their members. Do not look around to see if someone might need to know about Jesus. They will contaminate you. There is only one focus—obey the rules. It doesn't really matter if another church member is walking beside you. They are supposed to have the same focus as you, so both of you should look straight ahead. If you are both doing it correctly, communication will be difficult. There is no poking your head out.

Are you a turtle?

Romans 115:8 (NLT)

"And those who make idols are just like them ..."

Headphones and Spotters

FROM MY SEAT IN the grandstands I could see the entire racetrack and I was ready—sunblock, sunglasses, hat, and scanner headphones. I didn't want to miss anything.

To my right, at the very top of the bleachers, stood a row of men. I could see their silhouette against the blue sky. Soon I would hear their voices. They were the spotters. For each of them, it was their job to continually watch the action going on all around one car—the car and driver they worked for. Since there were 43 cars in the race, the row was comprised of 43 men.

The cars began to move and the voices in the headphones started their instructions. Some spotters talked a lot, others only when necessary. They gave information, like the distance from the car in front of them, the car behind them, or who was coming up on the outside. Instructions were given for how many laps left before pitting, how much fuel they had left, and who would be pitting with them.

I was listening to the 2 car when the spotter gave his driver this warning. "The 24 is waiting for the 15 to come by so he can take him out. Try to avoid them."

Sure enough, the 24 slammed into the 15, with two more cars piling in. But the 2 car drove around on the inside and avoided the wreck.

As I sat there, it occurred to me that I have a Spotter—one whose focus is entirely on me and what is happening in my life. If I listen to Him, He will keep me informed of how I'm doing in this race of life.

And He will help me avoid the wrecks, if I just listen.

Psalm 25:4 (NLT)
"Show me the right path, O Lord; point out the road for me to follow."

Debris in Your Lap

I WATCHED THE TELEVISION in horror as the car slammed into the safety barrier and disintegrated before my eyes. When the spinning cars all came to a stop, the front end of car 32 was missing. The flaming engine lay behind the barrier in the grandstand. Who knew where the tires were.

As the scene unfolded at the end of the Nationwide Race, my thoughts turned to another race, one I had attended. I sat on row 20, several yards before the finish line, exactly where the debris from this wreck had landed. Later, the news reported that one of the tires had landed in the lap of an unsuspecting spectator.

It could have been me.

I read comments that asked: "Why didn't they just get out of the way?"

How fast can you move in three seconds?

Those cars are going almost 200 mph. You have no warning. Suddenly you have debris in your lap.

Life is exactly like that. Our days are flying by with exciting activities and boring cautions. We are spectators.

And then suddenly we have debris in our lap.

A child is killed in a car crash.

A parent has a heart attack.

You are given a cancer diagnosis.

There is no escape. You just can't move fast enough.

Even though you may have debris in your lap, there is a Safety Barrier that will protect your soul. No matter how fast the oncoming crisis, that Barrier never breaks, keeping you safe.

John 10:28-29 (MSG)
"They are protected from the Destroyer for good. No one can steal them from out of my hand. The Father who put them under my care is so much greater than the Destroyer and Thief. No one could ever get them away from Him."

The Rookie Won

I always enjoy watching the Daytona 500—forty-three cars, five hundred miles, at a track where the race has occurred for fifty-three years. Many of the drivers have driven on that track for years; therefore, they know it well. But one year, things were different. The track was newly paved, and the cars had been reconfigured, which resulted in a totally new way of running the race. Drivers who found a *dancing partner* could go ten mph faster than a single car.

I listened to Darrell Waltrip, a past winner of the Daytona 500, who had driven on that track many times, as he described what was happening to the veteran drivers. They had to adjust to a whole new way of driving.

But there was a rookie in the mix. Trevor Bayne had never been in that race before. Saturday had been his birthday and he turned twenty. He had no preconceived ideas of how the race should go. He did not have to unlearn anything.

He won the race—the youngest driver to ever win it.

It was inspiring to hear him pray with his crew before the race, and to give God the glory when he won.

I thought of some of the churches I've been in. They are settled in their routine of how they "do" church. A new person comes in and the church immediately begins telling the new attendee how church works. Sometimes the young Christian will accept the teachings as fact, letting their new found enthusiasm be drained away by the rules and regulations of "doing it right."

But some are like Trevor Bayne. They turn to God for guidance. As they travel in new territory, they keep their eyes focused on the goal, winning the race.

As we listened to Trevor from his in-car audio, his excitement was contagious. That's the kind of Christ follower I desire to be—contagious in my love for Him.

Romans 12:11 (NIV)
"Never be lacking in zeal, but keep your spiritual fervor, serving the Lord."

The Goal

THE SEATTLE SEAHAWKS WERE playing the New Orleans Saints. Everyone knew the Saints were going to win, but people watched the game anyway. The Saints scored and heads were nodded. Yep. That's how it was going to be.

My husband and I went to Costco. Folks were talking about the game. The Seahawks were ahead. Huh?

When we got home, we turned on the television just in time to see Marshawn Lynch (someone I had never heard of) run 67 yards for a touchdown. The clip of that run was played and replayed. Lynch fought off seven tackles before crossing the goal line.

The Seahawks won the game.

The sermon at church the next morning began with that illustration. Lynch was focused on one thing—the goal line.

As a Christ follower, I want to be that focused on one thing, being Christ-like. But each day, I am tackled by impatience, pride, a judgmental attitude, etc.

I watched the replay as Lynch twisted, jumped, and pushed his way past those tackles. He was in great physical condition and could handle them.

To be able to handle my reactions to the things that tackle me in life, I need to be in great spiritual shape. Reading the Bible, praying, listening to biblical teaching, these are ways that enable me to stay focused on the goal—being Christ-like.

Philippians 3:13-14 (MSG)
"Friends don't get me wrong: By no means do I count myself an expert in all of this, but I've got my eye on the goal, where God is beckoning us onward—to Jesus. I'm off and running, and I'm not turning back."

So You Think You've Had a Bad Day

I ONCE VISITED A middle school, spending the day with the students. As I drove to the school, I pondered what I could say that would relate to kids their age.

My morning had not gone well, which resulted in me arriving late, but I was greeted enthusiastically and presented with gifts—Chai tea and tasty treats.

I had an "*aha*" moment.

My talk began with how my morning had gone wrong but ended well with gifts and time with them. Then I shared about my life—unwanted by my mother, married while still in high school, which was a life not of my choosing and ended in divorce. But years into my life, I met and married a wonderful man, and together we built a home and lived a truly blessed life.

"Just because you are having a bad life now does not mean it has to stay that way. When you arrive at an age that you can make choices for yourself, you can turn your life around."

Then I asked them to write me a little story about a bad day they had, or about a bad life they were living. Some of the stories broke my heart. A dad with a bullet in his heart. Children taken from their beds in the middle of the night and placed in foster care. Trying to sleep with people screaming and guns firing. A mother telling a girl that she didn't want her and was giving her away, but would keep the new baby because she loved it.

Out of 56 stories, 13 were about children trying to live their lives in a broken world, just wanting someone to love them. It's the only life they know.

When you think you are having a bad day, remember those kids.

Matthew 25:36 (MSG)

"I was hungry and you fed me, I was thirsty and you gave me a drink, I was homeless and you gave me a room, I was shivering and you gave me clothes, I was sick and you stopped to visit, I was in prison and you came to me."

Storm Cells in Life

My eyes were glued to the radar screen on my iPad. The color had changed from light green to darker green to yellow to orange to red and then purple. A storm front was moving across Alabama, traveling to Georgia. I watched as the cells grew in size and darkened. One was headed straight to where my daughter lived. And it was moving rapidly.

I called her. The air was full of noise—wind, rain and sirens. She had no shelter in which to take cover. The best she could do was an inner bathroom with no windows. I knew if that cell reached her, the bathroom would not save her.

As it darkened even more, it moved to within 20 miles of her, headed east and traveling 60 mph. It wouldn't be long. I could not help her. But God could. So, we prayed and placed her in God's hands. And then she calmly baked cookies for her cookie ministry.

I continued to watch the radar as she gave me the blow by blow of what was happening. The power went out. There were thuds against the building. It seemed to me the cell was moving between where she lived and Columbus. In my heart I knew people were dying as it moved along. I prayed for everyone.

As the cell moved past her and lightened in color, I knew the worst was over. We said a prayer of thankfulness for her, but my heart ached for those who had been hit.

And then the reports began coming in. Final total: 23 people dead.

As I watched the tragedy unfold, my thoughts turned to God. His viewpoint is much larger than my little iPad. How His heart must break when he sees the scenarios that occur in our lives as we leave Him out. He longs to protect us, and He offers security to us as our storms hit.

He's there and ready to help, if we turn to Him.

Matthew 7:26-27 (NIV)

"But everyone who hears these words of mine and does not put them into practice is like a foolish man who built his house on sand. The rain came down, the streams rose, and the winds blew and beat against that house, and it fell with a great crash."

My Part and God's Part

FOR SEVERAL YEARS I'VE had issues with too much acid in my esophagus. So, I've been given a list of foods to avoid. (Chocolate is in the list.)

One September, my husband and I took two trips—one to the ocean and one to Boise. It's hard to eat correctly while traveling. October included two more trips, this time for business, to San Diego and then Tulalip (that's in Washington). Then came Thanksgiving, my birthday, Christmas, etc. The list was pushed to the back of my mind.

Well, a few days later, the list moved to front and center. I was in pain.

As I drove to work, my conversation with God went something like this:

"God, I ask that you touch me. I know you are able to do that."

He gently reminded me that I had eaten badly, repeatedly.

"So how do I pray? How do I ask you to touch me when the distress is my own fault?"

He was still there, listening.

"OK, I get it. If I do my part, then I'll leave the rest up to you. Please help me do my part."

The next day I was better. I had chocolate covered almonds (a birthday present) sitting on my desk at work. I just looked at them.

A co-worker went to McDonald's for lunch. McDonald's made an error and gave him two orders of French fries. Those fries are my favorite, but I said "no" when offered the other order.

I struggled to do my part and left the rest to God.

Matthew 6:16-18 (MSG)

"When you practice some appetite-denying discipline to better concentrate on God, don't make a production out of it ... If you go into training inwardly, act normal outwardly ... God doesn't require attention-getting devices. He won't overlook what you are doing; he'll reward you well."

Look Around

ONE DAY IN CHURCH, I sat in front of a man who was carrying an oxygen tank and had the little hose prongs in his nose. There was a *swish-swish* sound each time the machine gave him some oxygen. As I listened to the rhythm of his life-saving air, I felt so very grateful for my health.

I was facing a medical test that week. Of course it had been on my mind. I would have a monitor hooked to me for 48 hours, but how could I whine about that, when he will (unless he is healed) have to carry his oxygen the rest of his life?

I also knew that he had buried his son two weeks previously. More reasons for me to be thankful. No parent should have to attend their own child's funeral.

If you are feeling down, look around. You can always find someone worse off than you.

Colossians 3:15 (NASB)
"Let the peace of Christ rule in your hearts, to which indeed you were called in one body; and be thankful."

Sending Signals

THERE WAS A CAPSULE attached to the inside of my esophagus. It was placed there to send signals to a monitor I carried for 48 hours. Even after I returned the monitor to the doctor, the capsule lingered on ... sending signals to the aliens, I guess.

I had been told I wouldn't be able to feel it (big untruth) and that it would release and pass through me (lovely) in 5-7 days. This little piece of equipment affected the way I breathed, swallowed, coughed, sneezed, and slept. I was aware of it constantly. Even though I tried not to think about it, it was always there, in the background.

At midnight on the last night, the capsule decided to move. I was wide-awake for 45 minutes, pondering my insides.

Sin is like that. It affects everything. Even though we try to ignore it, the results of sin are evident in our lives. And as we sin, we are sending signals to the people around us. If we say we are a Christ follower, they will be very aware of our hypocrisy.

As we live in this world, there will always be sin. But one of these days, whether through death or rapture, all sin signals will fall away. God will see each of us for exactly who we are on the inside—no monitor required.

Today, and every day, I need to focus on my actions with the same awareness that I had of that little capsule.

Psalm 51:10 (MSG)
"... give me a clean bill of health, God, make a fresh start in me ..."

Saying No

THE CHURCH NEEDED A kindergarten teacher for Sunday school and the finger was pointed at you. You had no choice. Suddenly you were the kindergarten teacher. Or maybe you were selected for the choir. Be there on Tuesday for practice. No questions—you would be there. And don't forget, Friday is church cleaning day and you are selected for that honor. Of course you show up.

Saying "no" is a sin.

At least, that was the training I received when I grew up, which ended with me being told whom I would marry and when.

I didn't want to sin.

Then my husband left, my church kicked me out, and my family (except for two long distance brothers) bombarded me with accusations. I had no friends, so was alone in my distress.

For two years I searched and researched, read and prayed. Some changes needed to be made. I learned to say "no".

Was I going to eat a second plate full of all that food? Or would I buy a bag of M&M's and eat them all? "Just say no" became my motto. I lost 100 pounds.

No longer would I teach kindergarten class just because I was told to. What if I was cantankerous and really didn't like little kids? Lots of harm would be done to their moldable spirits.

If I couldn't carry a tune in a bucket, then why would I be in the choir?

And if I needed to work four jobs to keep the bills paid and food on the table, then someone else could clean the church.

Saying "no" is hard for some people, but I got it down pretty well. Just ask my children.

When it was mentioned to one of my daughters that I never told her "no," she replied, "That's because I already know the questions that have a 'no' answer and I don't ask them."

What do you need to say "no" to? It's OK. Go ahead and say it.

Exodus 18:17 (MSG)
"This is no way to go about it. You'll burn out and the people right along with you. This is way too much for you ..."

Microcosm of Humanity

I WAS PEOPLE WATCHING in Seattle, with humanity flowing all around me. My husband, John, and I sat in the Ferry Terminal waiting to board. Next to us was the typical American young couple with two-year-old twins—boy and girl—with red hair. Adorable.

As we traveled from Seattle to Bremerton, we walked to the front of the ferry. One lady stood alone on the deck, facing forward, her hair standing straight out in the wind.

What is her story?

On the Bremerton side, waiting for the return ferry, the people got more interesting. A very classy older couple arrived. Maybe they lived in Bremerton and were attending an event in Seattle that evening.

The very mismatched couple caught my attention. She seemed to be trying to emulate Lady Gaga with her looks, and he was a mountain man. His jeans looked dirty, and he had a beard down his chest and a knit cap on his head.

I heard a tapping sound and turned to see a tall, slender, older man. He was dressed in neatly pressed jeans, a khaki jacket, and sunglasses. The tapping came from his white cane.

He obviously isn't going on a ferry for the scenery.

Just past the blind man stood a young couple holding hands. According to the size of her stomach, she was near her due date. They only had eyes for each other.

Two young men—one white and one black—walked up beside us. The white guy began asking me questions. "Is this where you line up for the ferry? Do I need a ticket?"

And then he said, "I'll be right back. I'm going to the restroom."

A younger man walked past. His face was painted blue.

Is he going to the Blue Man Group performing at the Paramount?

A young man wearing a baseball cap, with dreadlocks flying around his head, carried a cardboard sign making a statement about Corporate Greed. On his back was a bongo drum. Apparently, he was headed to the protests going on at Westlake Park.

Last, but not least, was the most unusual of the bunch. We heard him ~~coa~~ching from behind us, talking on a cell phone. Imagine my surprise ~~h~~e passed us wearing a hot pink blouse and a black sequined skirt, its tiers of ruffles reaching mid-calf on his legs. His long hair was gathered in a ponytail and, as he passed, I could see he needed a shave.

I had witnessed a microcosm of humanity. Each one has a story. And God knows each story in minute detail.

He also knows yours and mine.

Matthew 10:29-31 (NIV)

"Are not two sparrows sold for a penny? Yet not one of them will fall to the ground outside your Father's care. And even the very hairs of your head are all numbered. So, don't be afraid; you are worth more than many sparrows."

Don't Stink it Up

WHO TAKES OUT THE garbage at your house? Do you wait until the can is overflowing? Do you stick your foot in and smash it down so more garbage can fit in? If left too long, and with certain kinds of garbage, it will begin to stink up the house.

Do you have some personal garbage you need to take out, or have you been smashing it down pretending it's not there? Don't stink up your life with leftover garbage.

There can be many kinds of garbage in our bag—holding on to resentment, unforgiveness, or maybe wanting revenge for a wrong done. You get the picture.

How heavy is your garbage bag?

If you fail to break free of these barriers of the past, every day will be just like the last, still going in circles. For instance, in the Bible when God led the Hebrew people out of Egypt, they headed for the Promised Land. That was an 11-day journey.

But it took them 40 years!

Instead of moving forward with an attitude of faith, expecting good things, they went in circles, focusing on their problems, always complaining, and fretting about the obstacles standing between them and their destiny. They had to let go of past hurts, pains and failures before they could move on.

Don't let your past determine your future.

No matter what you've gone through, no matter how many setbacks you've suffered, and no matter who or what has tried to thwart your progress, you have a new day before you. Don't stink it up.

Only you can know the garbage you are carrying around, and only you can take it out.

Matthew 5-13 (MSG)
"Let me tell you why you are here. You're here to be salt-seasoning that brings out the God-flavors of this earth. If you lose your saltiness, how will people taste godliness? You've lost your usefulness and will end up in the garbage."

Chaff

I COULDN'T SHAKE THE word out of my head—chaff. It had been planted there at the Good Friday service. That evening, there had been eight stations around the edge of the auditorium. Each station was designed to help you contemplate your life. One had been a very simple spot against the wall—a table with some fans sitting on it to signify blowing away the chaff in our lives. Some written words helped direct our thinking.

Did I have chaff in my life?

That question stayed with me through the coming days.

The dictionary told me that chaff meant something comparatively worthless. So I began observing my daily routine and habits.

Boy, did I have chaff in my life.

How many programs on television are really worth watching? What kind of books do I read that bring value to my life? How much time do I waste on Facebook? What about my Bible reading and prayer time?

These were the questions in my head.

I needed to re-prioritize some activities.

As I evaluated my patterns, I realized this had to happen on the inside before I could make it work. If I truly desired change, I would see things with a new perspective. It was about the actions that others don't really see.

I've got a little fan that's blowing in my life, and it's helping to rid me of that chaff.

Ephesians 4:24 (MSG)
"And then take on an entirely new way of life—a God-fashioned life, a life renewed from the inside and working itself into your conduct as God accurately reproduces his character in you."

After Effects

I HAD KNOWN THEM FOR over two decades. When my husband and I moved to the Tri-Cities, we ended up attending the same church they did. I sang in choir and attended church functions with them.

He had a smile that went from ear to ear.

For several years I lost touch with them. We both changed churches. But after some time, we again landed in the same church. Once again, I was in choir with them.

He worked at the Hanford site. In the mornings, before work, some of the employees would gather on the grass to do stretching exercises. Many days they were so busy swatting mosquitoes that exercise was impossible, so they moved to an asphalt area to get away from the insects.

He was diagnosed with West Nile virus. Then he developed encephalitis, an infection of the brain, and was hospitalized for ten days. Some days he could go to work, other days he was readmitted to the hospital. They traveled to other cities seeking expert medical advice for his lingering symptoms.

Even though it was obvious to others he was still in distress—very thin and the smile gone—he continued to be active in choir. As Easter approached, I sat in front of him as we practiced the songs for the service.

Not long after that, he was not at practice. You see, he had taken his life the previous Monday.

We sat in a circle and cried, prayed, and told stories remembering him.

It was hard to think of other things. His death rearranged my priorities. I don't want to forget that life is very short. We never know if we will see that person again.

Give them a hug.

Tell them you love them.

Reach out in some way to help them feel someone cares.

And sometimes that is just not enough.

Psalm 23:4 (MSG)
"Even when the way goes through Death Valley, I'm not afraid when you walk at my side."

Dead ... or Alive

A TOMB WAS A HOME for the dead—a totally dark space of various sizes. After the body was placed in the tomb, it was wrapped in linen that had been saturated with embalming ointment—a mixture of myrrh and aloes. This ointment would then dry into a shellac-like substance and the linen wrap would become stiff. The body now resided in a hardened cocoon. If a large stone was rolled in front of the opening, that would make it much more difficult to move the body, making the burial site permanent.

Sometimes soldiers stood guard to protect the tomb from anyone who would attempt to touch or remove its contents. Every three hours, new guards arrived to replace the old ones.

I listened to Chuck Swindoll's podcasts on the crucifixion and burial of Jesus. As I pondered his words, I saw a correlation between the ancient tombs and the one I grew up in.

There was a lot of darkness and no life in the two rooms I called home. That lifelessness spilled over into the church we attended. The somber faces of the congregation gave the appearance of being shellacked into a hardened substance. With the stiffness of their spirits and an abundance of judgmental attitudes, the church members lived in a cocoon, never emerging and never allowing anyone in.

The black book we called "The Manual" could be compared to the large stone that was rolled across the doorway. And there were guards everywhere reporting my activities to anyone who would listen. They also brought in a fierce and frightening God. Knowing He was watching every move I made kept me securely entombed.

In my 30s, I discovered a different God who rolled the stone from my door.

Are you dead or alive? Tombs can come in all sizes and shapes—low self-esteem, alcoholism, abuse, drugs, and many other things can trap you in a very dark place. If you want out, there is a loving, caring God who will roll your stone away.

John 20:1 (NLT)
"Early on Sunday morning, while it was still dark, Mary Magdalene came to the tomb and found that the stone had been rolled away from the entrance."

Memories of May

GATHER CONSTRUCTION PAPER, TAPE, colors, scissors, flowers, and candy. Now you are ready to make a May basket. Cut off one end of the colored piece of paper to make a handle for the basket. Next, make the other piece of paper into the shape of a cone, with the bottom all closed in so nothing can fall through. The candy goes in first, and then flowers sit in the top part of the cone. The strip that was cut is made into a loop and taped to the top of the cone.

Oh, I forgot. If you want a design on your cone, you draw that on before you make the basket.

My nieces and I delivered May baskets in both pouring rain and in beautiful sunny weather. Using the handle loop, we placed the basket on the doorknob, rang the doorbell, and then ran. Such fun.

Years later, when I had three little girls, we made May baskets. They were far more creative than my childhood ones. And we made more memories.

Nowadays, some front doors don't have a doorknob. Where would you hang the basket? And many houses have a camera, so there would be no surprise as to who delivered it.

Another memory is the Maypole dance. Streamers hanging down from a pole and each participant would take hold of one streamer. Half of the kids were to go around the pole one direction, while the other half went in the other direction. As the music played, we intertwined the streamers, making a pattern on the pole. Each time we went around, it caused the pattern to cover the pole from top down and the streamers to get shorter. When we could no longer walk standing up straight, our Maypole dance was over.

I'm not sure you get the same kind of quality memories watching television or playing a video game together. Or maybe I'm of a different generation that finds no value in those activities.

How do you spend the 1st May? Make it special.

Psalm 46:8 (MSG)

"Attention all! See the marvels of God! He plants flowers and trees all over the earth."

Independence Day

AMERICANS CELEBRATE INDEPENDENCE DAY on the 4th of July. Independence did not come easily. Lives were lost and hardships endured. But today, we are no longer under the rule of Britain, thanks to our courageous forefathers.

As I pondered our Independence Day celebrations, my thoughts turned to my personal Independence Day. I didn't decide to fight for it. I was just suddenly in a battle that I didn't even understand. And just as the American Revolution lasted a few years, so too did my personal battle.

I had enemies I had never been aware of. They looked like friends and family. I had lived under their rule my whole life and did not realize I could escape. Therefore, I never tried.

One day, lying in a hospital bed, I reached an epiphany. My life did not have to be this way—ill and beaten down. Winning my war did not come easily. There were casualties along the way, as those friends and family did not care for the changes. My church kicked me out.

But there is a Book that is full of words declaring my independence. It wasn't written by Thomas Jefferson. No, the author of my Declaration of Independence is God, and it was signed by Jesus. He removed my chains of slavery and set me free.

I should light fireworks every day.

John 8:32 (MSG)
"If you stick with this, living out what I tell you, you are my disciples for sure. Then you will experience for yourselves the truth, and the truth will free you."

Boxed In

THE LAST WEEKEND IN July, our town hosts an annual event called the Water Follies. Thousands of people come from all over the Northwest to watch the Hydroplane races on the Columbia River. Upstream a little way is Art in the Park. Vendors set up booths and show their wares.

One year, my husband John and I timed our arrival to be at the park when they opened. We knew of a back way into a gravel parking lot that is close by the park, for easy access.

As John pulled into an empty spot on the exterior of the lot, I wondered about those cars choosing to park in the middle. How did they know where the available rows were? What would happen if someone parked in front and behind them?

Our perusal of Art in the Park didn't take long. In a little over an hour we had seen all we wanted to explore. As we walked toward the parking lot, I could see police cars and one woman. She was standing beside a car in the middle of the lot, with a car blocking her from behind and another keeping her from pulling forward. The center of the lot contained three rows. No one in that center row was going anywhere.

As we drove home, I pondered those boxed in cars. Shouldn't people have enough sense to know that the car they parked in front of wouldn't be able to get out if it already had a car behind it?

Then my thoughts turned inward. I know what it feels like to be boxed in. With the church on one side and my mother on the other, I had no freedom to move anywhere. I survived in the same mental, emotional, and spiritual spot for 30 years. By that age, I had already boxed in my own children. Wasn't that the way it was done?

No police arrived to make me allow them freedom of movement. Instead, God gently and quietly showed me the damage being done by my behavior and that I was inflicting the same pain I had endured. I removed my barriers and helped them make choices regarding their lives. They were no longer boxed in.

It is so easy to think we are keeping them safe, doing it for their own good, or that we know better. And sometimes we do. But many of the barricades we erect around our children are designed to make us feel better—to feel good about our parenting, to ensure they become whom we have chosen.

Is anyone boxed in because of you?

Romans 7:5 (MSG)

"When Christ died, he took that entire rule-dominated way of life down with him and left it in the tomb, leaving you free to 'marry' a resurrection life and bear 'offspring' of faith for God."

Patriotism

I RECENTLY READ THE book *Unbroken* by Laura Hillenbrand, a true story about World War II. It shares in detail what it was like to be a prisoner of war. The book is an almost unbelievable epic about what the human body and mind can endure.

As I read the pages, my thoughts turned repeatedly to my own brother. He was in that war, yet I've never heard him mention it. What I learned from him was the strong sense of patriotism I have today.

No, America does not have it all together. There are times I just shake my head in disbelief at some of the activities of the American people. I know all of that, but I still believe in the basic goodness on which country is founded.

It breaks my heart when I watch the news and see the maimed young people returning from war, but they did return. Others gave their lives. Yet when these returnees are interviewed, they tell us they would do it again—fight for their country. One man was recently killed during his 14th tour of duty. No one made him do that.

Deep within us is an allegiance to the concept of freedom. I've never been asked to give my life for that belief. Therefore, I acknowledge those who have been willing to go in my place, to protect my freedom.

Thank you.

Deuteronomy 20:1 (NLT)
"When you go out to fight your enemies and you face horses and chariots and an army greater than your own, do not be afraid. The Lord your God, who brought you safely out of Egypt, is with you!"

I Have Jesus

CHRISTMAS—WHEN WE CELEBRATE the birth of that little Baby. But sometimes the true meaning of Christmas gets lost in the shuffle of shopping, decorating, parties, and family gatherings.

A few years ago, something happened that made the birth of that Baby take on a whole new meaning.

We had a small group of people who met in our home every week. Norm, Anne, and their teenage daughter, Danielle, were a part of our little church family.

That was the year Anne and Danielle were murdered in their home.

Our small group took charge of feeding the family that gathered. Each day, John and I delivered their evening meal.

The tragedy occurred on a Monday. On the following Thursday, we sat with Norm on a back deck of the house where he was staying. As we shared and listened, he began to talk of peace—his peace. And then he said the words that so impacted my life: "I have Jesus."

That says it all.

That's why that little Baby was born.

John 14:27 (NIV)
"Peace I leave with you; my peace I give you. I do not give to you as the world gives. Do not let your hearts be troubled and do not be afraid."

Coming Up for Air

As I walked on the elevated track above the swimming pool, I noticed the scenario unfolding below me. A father was apparently trying to teach his young son to swim. Holding the buttocks of his son under his armpit with the body facing downward, he screamed, "Breathe, Chris," and then plunged the boy's face under water and held it there. The young boy's arms would flail, but he was no match against his father. When Dad decided his son had been underwater long enough, he would twist the child's face to the air. Chris cried and begged his dad to stop.

I yelled at the man to stop. He continued.

Long story short: I reported it to the front desk. They called the police. The father was arrested. I wrote a detailed report and he was banned from the gym.

I used to feel a little like Chris at Christmas time. I was bound by the rules and regulations of what it meant to be proper. Decorations needed to look a certain way and be put up by a certain time. Gifts were to be purchased for more than family; anyone who might have talked to you in the past year was eligible. The wrappings were to look like something out of a magazine.

The Christmas cards, elegant and pricey, were to be mailed in time to be received before Christmas. You got extra points for being the first one. Each one had to be handwritten with a lovely comment inside. Some blank cards were set aside to take care of those people who sent you a card and you hadn't sent them one.

Every time I tried to come up for air, I was plunged back under.

Today, Christmas no longer has me in its clutches. When I see something I think someone might like, even in June, I purchase it and give it to them—in June. My decorations have a central theme—the nativity. I add a few more pieces each year. I still send some Christmas cards, but it is no longer a competition.

Come up for air, breathe and savor the birth we celebrate.

Luke 2:10-11 (NLT)

"I bring you good news that will bring great joy to all people. The Savior—yes, the Messiah, the Lord—has been born today in Bethlehem, the city of David!"

Going Against the Flow

I've read that people gain at least six pounds during the holidays. I've proven that true year after year. Yep, I gained again this year during Thanksgiving time. Then my birthday rolled around and I ate cookies. Lots of them. I like cookies. Next on the agenda was a party at our house with an abundance of food.

I made a decision. I would not eat at the party. I didn't quite make it. I ate some bread with spinach and artichoke dip. Three days later was the potluck at my work with lots of good stuff. I remembered my decision and ate sparingly.

I'm down three pounds since then.

I know that doesn't sound like much, but to me it is huge.

It is extremely difficult to go against the flow—peer pressure, cravings, and wanting to fit in. And I like to eat, especially all the wonderful desserts.

Being a Christ-follower is like that. It requires a decision. It is much easier to just go with the flow. The peer pressure, cravings, and the need to join in all lead to a life of following the crowd. And just because we have decided to be different doesn't make it easy. As Christ-followers, we still slip and fall.

But it feels good to know that Christ knows our intent. He understands about slipping and falling.

Proverbs 1:18-19 (MSG)

"Nobody robs a bank with everyone watching, yet that's what these people are doing—they're doing themselves in. When you grab all you can get, that's what happens: the more you get, the less you are."

Here I Am ... Again

I AM AN OVER-EATER. Weight has always been an issue for me. In the 1970s I lost almost 100 pounds. But if you made a graph of my weight loss and weight gain, it would look like a road map of hills.

And here I am again.

I've made it through the holidays with a loss of five pounds. But before I pat myself on the back, I've been at this weight before, many times. Even if I lose ten more pounds, that's still just one of those valleys I've gone through before the chart goes up again.

Sometimes living a Christian life is like that.

A while ago, Chuck Swindoll asked, "Are you spending more time reading the newspaper than you are reading the Bible?" I had to say "yes." I really enjoy reading *USA Today*, so I subscribed. Convicted by my "yes" answer, I canceled my subscription.

I purchased a CD study series on Proverbs from *Insight for Living*. Proverbs is full of wisdom and practicality, but it was up to me to make the time in my schedule to sit down and actually listen and study.

I've been here before. It seems so simple to just eat less, and some of you reading these words will loudly agree. You've never struggled with your weight. But I know there are some of you who understand exactly what I'm saying. It's so much more than just opening your mouth and putting food in.

It's the same with growing as a Christian. It isn't a complicated plan to make time in your day for the Bible. But when it comes right down to it, it's such a struggle to find that quiet time, that place alone where you can focus, listen, and learn.

I can't say I hunger for food, but I do hunger for the Word. I want to ingest it and have it become a part of me. I desire to reach a deeper place with God.

Just as eating requires an opening of my mouth, reading and understanding the Word requires an opening of my heart and mind.

And here I am ... again.

John 6:35 (MSG)
"Jesus said, 'I am the Bread of Life. The person who aligns with me hungers no more and thirsts no more, ever.'"

He's Not a Cop

I PULLED TO A STOP at the red light, glancing in my rearview mirror. That's when I saw it. Behind me was a police car. Instantly I was on the alert. *I have to do everything right or he'll pull me over.*

When the light changed, I turned left. So, did he. *Swell. I wonder how long he will be behind me?*

Glancing at my speedometer, I made sure I signaled before I changed lanes. He signaled to change lanes too. *This is nerve-wracking. When is he going to go somewhere else?*

At Columbia Center Boulevard, I turned right. He turned right. *I'm only halfway there. Is he going to follow me the whole way?*

When I changed lanes again, my shadow came with me. *So far, so good. No lights telling me to pull over.*

I pulled into the mall parking lot with him right behind me. I finally reached my destination and pulled into a parking space.

Only then did he leave me. Only then could I relax.

As I walked to meet my friend, I pondered the feeling I had when the policeman was behind me. It wasn't a good one—tense and wary. That's how I lived the first half of my life—tense and wary of God. I constantly lived with the feeling that God was right behind me, watching every move I made, ready to turn on His lights, pull me over and place me under arrest.

I'm so grateful I no longer believe that. He's not behind me, watching my every move. He is right beside me, sometimes carrying me, as I journey through this life.

Matthew 18:12-14 (MSG)
"Look at it this way. If someone has a hundred sheep and one of them wanders off, doesn't he leave the ninety-nine and go after the one? And if he finds it, doesn't he make far more over it than over the ninety-nine who stay put? Your Father in heaven feels the same way."

He Touched Me

HE LAID HIS HAND on my head. *I may never wash my hair again.* A nationally known musician, Rafael Mendez, was actually touching me.

My fifth-grade class had attended his concert and I had been enraptured by his rendition of *Flight of the Bumblebee.*

Then he invited the class to visit with him.

Mendez had recorded many records, appeared on television shows, and then began his fulltime career as a trumpet soloist, performing more than 100 concerts a year across the United States and Europe. But it was his strong sense of duty toward education that had allowed a bunch of school children to be his special audience.

And he had touched me.

As I think back to that day, I remember my feeling of awe. I was in the presence of a great man. I didn't wash my hair for a week, but in those days, you only washed your hair once a week. I remember thinking, *I'm washing off where he touched me.*

Have you ever been in the presence of a great person? Did that contact linger with you? Did you become a better person, just by being near them?

As I ponder these thoughts, my mind turns to my contact one day with Jesus. I hadn't really heard much about Him. My childhood was spent being taught about God—His power and how He would use that power to get you if you did something wrong. It would have been a fearful thing to be touched by Him.

But one day Jesus touched my heart and I've never been the same. Soap and water cannot make that contact go away. My awe and reverence are as strong today as they were all those years ago.

Mark 1:40-41 (MSG)

"A leper came to Him, begging on his knees, 'If You want to, You can cleanse me.' Deeply moved, Jesus put out His hand, touched him, and said, 'I want to. Be clean.'"

Never Give Up

GENE OROWITZ WAS A bed wetter into his adolescence. His mother regularly humiliated him by hanging his wet sheets out of his bedroom window for all his friends to see. She told him he would never amount to anything. His failure in high school seemed to bear her words out. He graduated 299th out of a class of 301.

Things didn't get much better for Gene after high school. Because he excelled in track, he was awarded a scholarship to the University of Southern California. He lost that scholarship during his freshman year because of a disappointing track season. He ended up sleeping on park benches in Santa Monica, California.

Yet, in terms of success, Gene went on to become the most successful television writer, director, and producer in television history. Gene Orowitz became the man we know as Michael Landon.

Perseverance. Do you have it?

In the sixties, if you were a guy in high school, the last place you wanted to be was in the band at the football game. Steve was a skinny, shy, clarinet player. No football for him. He wasn't a great student and considered a C minus to be a good grade. But today, his name has appeared on five of the top ten grossing films of all time. The world knows him as Steven Spielberg.

What would success look like to you?

Spending more time with your kids?

Being able to travel?

Is "I quit" in your vocabulary?

Probably the greatest example of perseverance is Abraham Lincoln. Born into poverty, he lost eight elections, failed twice in business, and suffered a nervous breakdown. After losing a senate race, Lincoln said, "The path was worn and slippery. My foot slipped from under me, knocking the other out of the way. But I recovered and said to myself 'it's a slip and not a fall.'"

And because he didn't quit, he became one of the greatest presidents in the history of our country.

Do you have goals you are trying to reach?

How long are you willing to work toward attaining them?

Do you have a way of measuring your success?

Today is a brand-new day.

Today I can choose to persevere.

How about you? What will be different for you and me in five or ten years because we didn't quit today?

Mark 13:13 (MSG)

"Stay with it—that's what is required. Stay with it to the end."

Jumping to Conclusions

In the Bible, in 1 Samuel 1, there is an interesting story about a woman named Hannah who had no children. Year after year people made fun of her, making her cry and unable to eat.

One time, Hannah went to the Tabernacle to pray, in deep anguish and crying bitterly. She made a vow that if God would give her a son, she would give him back to the Lord for his entire lifetime.

But there was a problem. Hannah was not praying out loud. She was just moving her lips.

Eli, the priest, was watching her. Seeing her lips move, but hearing no sound, he assumed she had been drinking and admonished her for it.

Oops. Even priests make mistakes.

Many times we jump to conclusions without first checking the facts. Then we tell someone else what we perceived and that is how gossip starts. Those unfounded rumors will some day make it back to the person we said them about.

It hurts badly to be the brunt of gossip. I speak from experience. Therefore, I do not want to inflict that kind of pain on someone else.

I ask God to put a guard on my lips.

Proverbs 10:18 (NLT)
"Hiding hatred makes you a liar; slandering others makes you a fool."

It's the Small Stuff that Gets Us

THE WEATHER FORECAST WAS for 6 to 8 inches of snow. I had to be at work early, but upon arising at 4:45, there was just a skiff of snow.

No problem.

So I followed my normal routine and went to the gym.

An hour later and the roads were covered, but still doable. I drove to work.

My office has no windows. Hard at work, it was an hour later when I glanced out the front windows. It resembled a blizzard out there. The flag across the street stood straight out.

Not good.

More work, and then another check on conditions. The flag was obscured by the snow. Reports began to trickle in—cars spinning out and highways closed.

I wanted to be home.

With the necessary work completed, I headed out. With a fierce grip on the steering wheel, I stayed focused on everything—road ahead, cars beside, and cars behind.

I traveled slowly through the streets. Not wanting to come to a complete stop at stop signs, I kept my wheels turning just a little, glancing in all directions. There weren't many cars on the road.

Roundabouts were tricky. They resembled skating rinks. My mind was constantly thinking ahead to the next obstacle I would face.

Finally, I was within blocks of my home. I turned into my street with my house up ahead. I pushed on the garage door opener. I was almost there.

As the door opened, I turned the car into the driveway, slowing down for the turn. Too slow. My tires were spinning.

Checking my rear-view mirror to make sure no cars were parked across the street, I put the car in reverse and backed out into the street. Going way too fast for my comfort, I gunned my way up the driveway.

It worked.

Life is so like that. There are obstacles everywhere. We need to be on the alert all the time—watching ahead, beside, and behind us—never knowing exactly when the next difficulty will arise. With that awareness, we keep our minds, bodies, and souls safe. Then we relax. Something as simple as our own driveway is certainly not an issue.

But that is when we are most vulnerable, when we think we've arrived.

1 Peter 5:8 (NASB)

"Keep a cool head. Stay alert. The Devil is poised to pounce and would like nothing better than to catch you napping. Keep your guard up."

My Capo D'Astro Bar

PIANOS HAVE A DEVICE called the Capo d'Astro Bar, which is a bar under the piano, fixed across the harp and bearing down on the strings. It is designed to prevent any warping. In most pianos, this device isn't heavy enough to actually prevent warping. But some have a heavy-duty metallic Capo d'Astro Bar.

The strings in a piano don't even begin to warp until 50 years have passed. That means for 50 years the Capo d'Astro Bar is just sitting there, waiting to be put to work.

When I learned of the Capo d'Astro Bar, I immediately drew a parallel to my life.

When I was about 30 years old, I made a wonderful discovery. I had been gifted from birth with a heavy-duty Capo D'Astro Bar. It had been there through all my hurting years, just waiting for the right moment to begin its job. At 30, it began working, pressing on my warping strings and bringing me into tune.

God is my Capo D'Astro Bar.

He waited patiently while I struggled through those early years.

He waited some more while I worked my way out of a life that had been programmed by others.

More waiting while I searched for the "real" me inside.

And when I chose to begin a new life, my Capo D'Astro Bar began doing the work it was designed to do.

This Bar will never break.

It will never need to be repaired.

There is no heavier Capo D'Astro Bar.

It will last forever.

What more could I ask?

I see people all around me who are having a problem with their warping strings. I want to open up their piano and show them the tinker toy bar they have inside, that will never keep them from warping. But they have to want a heavy-duty tune up. I didn't know I was out of tune for all those years, and just as God was patient with me, I must be patient with them.

The next time you listen to a piano being played, think about what is inside, pressing on the strings, keeping it in tune. Then turn your thoughts inward and check out your own Capo D'Astro Bar.

Do you have the heavy-duty one?

Is it still waiting to go to work?
Tinker toy or heavy-duty. The choice is up to you.

Proverbs 4:20 (MSG)

"Dear friend, listen well to my words; tune your ears to my voice."

He is Free

THERE IT WAS IN black and white—a name I knew. I stared at the newspaper page—26 years; such a long time. And now he was free.

My mind flew back 25 years and I could see that little boy, crawling among our legs as the church choir practiced.

Then the tragedy. He was found floating in the pool.

Drastic measures were taken. Machines had been used. Prayer groups met around the clock. Tears were shed. Such a darling little boy.

I visited the hospital. His grandma and I became friends as we worked his little arms and legs to prevent stiffening.

Weaned from the machines, he was discharged to go home. But everything was different now. He couldn't play with his toys, couldn't make a mess, and would never ride a bike or attend school.

Instead, he lay in his bed.

Teams of people signed up to help the family. Some brought meals. Others took their turn at moving his little limbs, keeping them limber. My heart broke each time it was my turn, eventually causing me to volunteer in a different way. I could do their ironing.

Their home was a scene of constant people in and out.

He still lay there.

Now he's free—running and laughing.

My emotions are a mix of sad and glad. As he lay there, he taught me so many lessons. Limited as his life was, it served a purpose.

For those of us who arise each morning with our faculties intact, much more is expected.

Revelation 21:4 (NLT)
"He will wipe every tear from their eyes, and there will be no more death or sorrow or crying or pain. All these things are gone forever."

Fearplugs

I'VE TRIED. I REALLY have. One block, two blocks ... but then my breathing becomes labored. Three blocks and I can't take any more. I begin to run away from the terrifying sound of the ocean.

I grew up in Kansas. No oceans.

It's the overwhelming noise. I've missed out on walks on the beach with my husband, with children, with friends. I compare my feeling of terror to what people running from a tsunami must feel, or those running from a wall of mud, or those who scream as a tornado rips a child from their arms. I can't describe the feeling.

Weeks before my husband and I went to the ocean for a few days with friends, I already knew I wouldn't like my behavior.

Earplugs were suggested, but I knew they wouldn't work. I would still know the ocean was there.

So I decided to begin praying for fearplugs.

There is something deep within me that is out of whack. If I knew what it was, I would fix it. But I know Someone who has a supply of fearplugs—plugs that restore calm. I have taken from that supply for many other situations in my life. I would do it again for this trip.

Matthew 8:25-26 (NLT)

"The disciples went and woke him up, shouting, 'Lord, save us! We're going to drown!' Jesus responded, 'Why are you afraid? You have so little faith!' Then he got up and rebuked the wind and waves, and suddenly there was a great calm."

Fearplugs Addendum

THE TIME FOR TERROR had arrived. My intestines let me know they didn't like this idea. Tears threatened. My heart rate accelerated. And we hadn't even reached the elevator to take us to the ground floor so we could walk to the beach.

Our friends, Phil and Anita, together with my husband John, were accompanying me on this journey. I knew John understood the depth of my fear, but it was difficult to make others realize the battle within me.

Their talk buzzed over my head. My focus was on taking the next step and the next one.

And then there it was, wave after wave rolling in. I could hear my heart beating in my ears, along with the roar. The tears flowed. I was so tired of this. I stopped walking and stood facing the ocean.

"I need you to pray."

So the prayers began and were completed.

Still, I stood facing my dreaded foe. I was ready to stand there for hours awaiting the calm.

Gradually my heart rate slowed and the tears dried up. I raised my head and stared at the restless movement. No clenching in my gut.

"OK, we can walk now."

Any time I have ever been to the beach, my spot in the line of people walking along the water's edge was the furthest away from the ocean. No logic there, but it gave me a buffer. Yet here I was, walking the closest to the water and actually carrying on a conversation. My brain was functioning again.

When we turned and headed back, I remained on the side next to the water. No tears. No pounding heart.

For me, the test would be the next time.

I'm delighted to say I returned to the beach with a smile on my face. Tears of gratitude, not fear, rolled down my cheeks. The raging tumult within me had been stilled.

Psalm 107:29-30 (NLT)
"He calmed the storm to a whisper and stilled the waves. What a blessing was that stillness ..."

Instant Gratification

I RUB A LITTLE butter on it, sprinkle some seasoning, poke some holes, wrap it in foil, and place it in the oven to bake. When the potato is removed from the oven it will melt in my mouth with tenderness. My favorite toppings are taco meat, shredded cheese, and sour cream. Delicious.

Or if you are an instant gratification type of person, just wrap it in Saran wrap and pop it in the microwave. In a few minutes you'll have an eatable potato, but you can never call it a baked one. And there is no way to compare the two.

I once placed some black beans, white beans, seasoning, a cup of chicken broth, and chunks of chicken breast in a Crockpot, stirred the mix and put on the lid. It simmered all day. The chicken was fall-apart tender, and it tasted wonderful.

Or if you are an instant gratification type, just go to your pantry and choose from the cans of soup you have there. Open the can, pour the contents into a bowl, and put it in the microwave. A few minutes later you will have hot soup, but there is no way to compare the two soups.

Credit cards are a great help when you are an instant gratification type. You see something you want and you buy it. When that card is maxed out, you can just get another one. The fact that you can't pay the card off every month does not seem to be an issue.

Instant gratification is not a new concept. There were people in Jesus' day who sought instant gratification, too. As He had ascended into heaven, the people were told He would return. But as the days and weeks passed, and He still had not come back, some followers, and all of the scoffers, were saying, "Jesus promised to come back didn't He? Then where is He?" (2 Peter 3:4 NLT)

They had forgotten that, to Jesus, a day is like a thousand years and a thousand years are like a day. Jesus is not being slow in His return. He is being patient for the sake of the one who has not yet believed.

Jesus is definitely not an instant gratification type.

Are you?

Acts 1:11 (NLT)
"Jesus has been taken from you into heaven, but someday he will return from heaven in the same way you saw him go!"

Hand-Me-Down Shoes

I GREW UP WEARING hand-me-down shoes. Whether they fit or not was never the issue. Did they cover my feet when it snowed? Did they prevent me from stepping on a sharp object? If so, they were doing their job. Therefore, I've lived with corns and bunions. Add to that information the fact that I have a very high arch, and that only increases the problems with my feet.

Buying shoes has never been fun, but slowly, over years of purchasing the correct size, the corns have disappeared. The bunion is a permanent fixture but does ache less.

One day I splurged. Instead of buying just any tennis shoe, I went to the experts (I think). The first thing they did was have me take off my shoes and stand on a piece of equipment that reminded me of the scale I weigh myself on at home. An image appeared on a screen showing the pressure points of my feet. Nothing showed between my heels and the balls of my feet.

Did I mention I have a high arch?

There, in living color, was the proof. I was told this is the foot type that needs the most assistance with shock absorption, since the rigid structure doesn't dispel impact forces very well. Nice.

I left the store wearing my new shoes designed specifically for me.

That illustration relates precisely to my religious experience. I grew up wearing my mother's religion. Did I attend church every time the doors were open? Did I keep myself separate from the evil in the world, its activities and people? If so, my religion was doing its job.

I developed all sorts of illnesses and mental hang-ups. No matter; they were badges of honor for doing the right thing.

Slowly, over the years, I began to see that maybe, just maybe, religion didn't fit me. Instead, I discovered an Expert who gently guided me into a relationship with a Person. I threw my mother's religion away and now a delightful Presence resides within me, designed specifically for me.

The same Expert is available for you.

Proverbs 8:30 (NIV)
"I was filled with delight day after day, rejoicing always in His Presence."

In the Movie Business

I REMEMBER HEARING ON the news one day about a man who accidentally called his wife's cell phone while he was killing her. The voice mail on her phone had a recording of him saying he was going to kill her and then her screams.

My Bible tells me everything I do in this life is being recorded. I forget that sometimes. But just as that man had no recourse when the tape was played for the jury, I will have no way to explain my way out of my wrong actions when I stand before God.

How big do you think the screen will be as it plays the movie of my life? As it plays out yours?

Revelation 20:13b (nlt)
"The sea gave up its dead, and death and the grave gave up their dead. And all were judged according to their deeds."

Imperfect Vessels

MY HUSBAND AND I had been to the coast for a few days. On our way home, we stopped at a sandwich shop for a bite to eat. When I walked through the doorway of the deli, my eyes immediately spied a display of mugs on two shelves. Not stopping to find a table or look at a menu, I walked straight to the shelves and took out my camera.

My husband joined me as I snapped the pictures. "Why are you taking pictures of these mugs?"

"There's a story here."

They all had something in common. They weren't normal shapes. Someone with a very creative mind had formed them.

I knew about misshapen mugs. I was one. Having been told many times by my mother I was a mistake; I had known from a very early age that I did not fit the mold for normal. As the years went by, it became very clear to me that I was not useful in society. I knew, deep inside, no one wanted to be around me. I was just an irregular piece of humanity.

When my first husband left me, I was forced to go out into the world. Selling Avon was not my forté, but I needed some kind of income and had no skills. With children counting on me, I couldn't go home and hide. As I drove from house to house and neighborhood to neighborhood, I had time to think.

I needed to do something about *me*.

I began to spend serious time looking at me and at the Bible. Imagine my surprise when I found a verse in there that spoke to my inner core. Colossians 1:27 says, "The mystery in a nutshell is just this: Christ is in you." (MSG)

It didn't matter if I was imperfect. I could still be a vessel. Just as the odd shaped mugs could still hold coffee or hot chocolate, I could contain Christ. Someone with a very creative mind had formed me. The shape didn't matter.

How very freeing that discovery was. All I needed to do was be the very best receptacle I could be. With Christ in me, who knew how far I could go?

Isaiah 45:9 (NLT)
"What sorrow awaits those who argue with their Creator. Does a clay pot argue with its Maker? Does the clay dispute with the One who shapes it, saying, 'Stop, you're doing it wrong!'"

I Know a Guy

THE CARTOON CAUGHT MY eye. Garfield was looking at a caterpillar crawling on the ground. The caterpillar tells Garfield, "I'm going to be a butterfly."

Garfield asks, "And just how are you going to do that?"

"I know a guy," the caterpillar replies.

That's when my mind took off.

Caterpillars are not lovely. They crawl along the ground. Sometimes they get stepped on, they are so vulnerable. Do they know that one day they will be beautiful? They are hungry little creatures, stuffing themselves. In the next stage they hang upside down and encase themselves with a shiny chrysalis. And here comes the fascinating part. While they are hanging upside down, inside their protective casing, they are being transformed.

I love the word "metamorphosis". It resonates with such rich meaning. The caterpillar knows a "guy".

I've spent time crawling along the ground and being stepped on. I had no idea that I contained the makings to become beautiful. But as I passed through the stages of my life, I became hungry—hungry to know more than just crawling along the ground.

It was not of my own doing that I became isolated inside a protective armor. But my time there was not wasted. Slowly, slowly, the transformation occurred.

I, too, know a Guy.

My loving Father caused a metamorphosis to occur. My ugly parts were discarded. Negativity turned into positivity. Judgments turned into empathy. Fear was replaced with peace. Laughter bubbled forth.

You, too, can know a Guy.

John 14:2-3 (NIV)
"Don't run roughshod over the concerns of your brothers and sisters ...
God hasn't invited us into a disorderly, unkempt life but into something
holy and beautiful—as beautiful on the inside as the outside."

I Didn't Tell Her

HER REAL NAME WAS Eva. But somehow that just didn't fit, so she was called Ernie. She came into my life when my husband and I became friends with her son and his wife. As our friendship grew, we were included as family on many occasions. How special that was to me, having been raised with a mother who didn't seem to know how to smile.

Ernie smiled.

They always had a costume party for Halloween. One year, Ernie and her children came dressed in wedding clothes. Her dress still fit.

We've watched the Super Bowl together, accepted as part of the group, and always eating wonderful food prepared by family.

She and her husband were the true patriarch and matriarch of that family line. I loved being around them. They laughed and loved and cared about each other. With her children, grandchildren and eventually great-grandchildren enjoying life all around her, she would sit observing. But she was never idle. Her hands were always busy with a knitting project.

Then the day came when I sat in the shade beside her by the swimming pool at her son's home. I had been told her cancer had returned and that this time the treatments would be easier. She wouldn't get so sick and her hair wouldn't fall out. But that day by the pool, cancer was not mentioned. We talked of life and love and happy things as her fingers flew, working on the ever-present project.

She gave no indication her life was in serious trouble. That's why it was such a shock when the text arrived a month later. Ernie had passed away.

My thoughts bounced around in my head. What will her husband do? What can we do? And in between all those other thoughts, one came repeatedly. I never told her that she was my role model for being a mom, a grandma, a great-grandma, and for facing the challenge of cancer without any grumbling or seeking pity.

I didn't tell her.

And so, I'm left to work through that. But if there is someone you want to say something to, do it.

James 4:14 (NIV)
"Why, you do not even know what will happen tomorrow. What is your life? You are a mist that appears for a little while and then vanishes."

I am a Bible

THE SOUND OF THE keyboard filled the meeting room. Our worship leader spoke as she played some background music. In her comments, she referred to a certain version of the Bible.

Later, after some songs, she again mentioned a scripture from a different version of the Bible.

And so it went for all the sessions.

There are many different versions of the Bible. The speaker read from a certain version and then compared it to a different version. Between the speaker and worship leader, probably four or five different versions of the Bible were read, plus some reading from *The Message* paraphrase.

Our ladies retreat was attended by various types of women: some non-Christians, some newly Christian, and some who had been Christians for years. No matter where they were on their journey, there was a Bible version that could speak to them.

But what about the people we come in contact with every day? They've probably never been to a Christian retreat. We work with them, live next door to them, and buy products from them. As I pondered the words read to me at the retreat, I remembered a saying: "You may be the only Bible some people read."

All the different versions of the Bible point to central truths. God loves you and desires a relationship with you. If we call ourselves Christians, shouldn't our lives point to the same truths? Our reactions to circumstances display a certain version of the Bible. Do we point to a loving God? Do our words line up with a God who understands us? Or do we demonstrate a life of judgment and condemnation?

What version are you?

Titus 2:5b (MSG)

"We don't want anyone looking down on God's Message because of their (our) behavior."

Holding Hands

MY HUSBAND JOHN AND I had been on our Friday night date—getting a bite to eat and going to a movie. We always held hands a lot.

As we left the movie, John was in front of me, squished in with all the other people headed toward the exit. I saw his hand reach back to take mine, but a man had come between us.

John kept trying to hold this guy's hand, while the guy kept swatting him away. I, of course, was doubled over laughing.

When the crowd dispersed, John asked, "Why wouldn't you take my hand?"

Due to my laughter, it took a while to tell.

There is Someone who is trying to take your hand. Do you keep swatting Him away? Maybe you've been told He is mean and does bad things to you, or makes you go to Africa and live in a jungle. Maybe you've never really understood who He is. You are afraid.

Take His hand. It's safe. He loves you and wants to go on a lot of dates with you. More than just Friday nights.

Romans 8:39 (MSG)

"Do you think anyone is going to be able to drive a wedge between us and Christ's love for us? There is no way!"

Headwaters

To my right, as John and I drove north toward Banff, Canada, I spotted a sign that said: *Columbia Lake.* Since I live in a city with the Columbia River flowing through it, the name caught my attention.

Soon, I noticed another sign to the left of the highway stating we were traveling along the Columbia River.

How cool. That river is flowing south and will go within blocks of my home.

We enjoyed our fabulous weeklong stay, even journeying to the Columbia Ice Fields, but my "duh" moment came at home when I studied the Canadian Rockies map I had purchased. That's when I noticed the Columbia River did not go south from Columbia Lake. It traveled northwest.

Research ensued.

From its headwaters at Columbia Lake, the river flows northwest for 200 miles through the Columbia Valley, including the ice fields. Then it turns sharply south, crossing the border into eastern Washington.

The Columbia River is the largest river in the Pacific Northwest, the fourth largest in the United States, and its course takes it all four directions.

How had I lived beside it for 27 years and not known that?

Yet how many people live for years within blocks of a church and have no idea that the headwaters of abundant life are available within?

The flow of God's grace is the largest in the universe and travels all directions. The Bible is available to anyone who is interested in understanding about that flow. It clearly shows the course of God's love.

As a Christ-follower, it is up to me to help others reach that "duh" moment when they are eager to discover more about the perpetual headwaters of life.

John 4:10 (MSG)
"Jesus answered, 'If you knew the generosity of God and who I am, you would be asking me for a drink, and I would give you fresh, living water.'"

Secure in Him

IT HAD BEEN A busy day. First, I met friends at Starbucks, then took myself to lunch followed by a movie. Returning home, I settled myself in my recliner to watch the Olympics. Then it was bedtime.

In the bathroom, ready to don my pajamas, I reached in my pants pocket to remove the device I have carried since John's death. Whether I am in my home or driving across the United States, as long as I am in cell phone range, that little black tool keeps track of my location. No matter what kind of emergency I may be undergoing, all I have to do is push the call button and help is on the other end. I've grown accustomed to that close security, but this time my pocket was empty.

I thought back over my day and wondered exactly when it had slipped out of my pocket. Starbucks? Restaurant? Movie Theater? Since I couldn't retrace those steps, I started with my recliner. Digging deep into the cracks below the cushions, I felt my way around. No device. I raised the leg portion and practically crawled under the chair to poke and prod some more. No luck.

The car also came up empty.

Now what was I supposed to do at eleven at night?

I reached for my housecoat. *Guess I'll just have to go to bed.*

But the housecoat felt a little heavy. My security device had been in its pocket all day, in my closet, doing me absolutely no good. Yet I had sensed no unease, secure in the knowledge I was protected.

Sometimes life is like that. We think we have a good friend, but then they don't connect with us. Somewhere along the way we've lost them and didn't even realize it. Or what about feeling secure in a job? Promotion time and someone else gets it. Is our job not so secure after all?

As a Christ-follower, I have no worries about my security in this life and after. He never falls out of my pocket or gets broken. He is just there, always, when I need Him.

I'm always secure in Him.

Psalm 91:11-12 (NIV)

"For he will command His angels concerning you to guard you in all your ways; they will lift you up in their hands so that you will not strike your foot against a stone."

It Happened Again

I WAS ON THE treadmill one morning when a "life lesson" happened.

I had recently purchased a new iPhone 8. A friend, who knows the tech language, went with me to answer the gigabyte and pixel questions. Once I had the new phone, my friend and his 12-year-old grandson traveled home with me to make sure I was all set up.

As my friend unpacked the accessories, he explained to his grandson what the short cord was for. "It's for when you want to listen to music on your iPhone. You plug one end into the phone and the other end is where you plug your ear buds."

I don't listen to music on my iPhone so paid no attention to his explanation.

Then came that morning when I stepped on the treadmill and placed my headphones on my head. It's my routine to listen to podcasts as I walk. I reached for my phone to plug them in, but there was no little hole to insert the headphone cord. I turned that phone upside down and back to front looking for the hole.

This is a new phone. My old phone had a place for the headphones. Why on earth would the new one not?

And then the light bulb came on. *Ahh! That little cord. That's what it's for.* Not just for music but for podcasts too.

That morning I walked in silence.

Life is like that. Many times, we don't really pay attention because we think it doesn't affect us. And then we discover it really does.

Do you know how to be around an autistic child? Until I became friends with someone who has an autistic child, I paid no attention to the articles and books on their differences. Once I knew I would be around one, I devoured information to help me understand not only the child but also what the parent was experiencing.

We never know when a "life lesson" will occur, but they are happening all around us. Plug in and pay attention.

Proverbs 24:32 (NIV)
"I applied my heart to what I observed and learned a lesson from what I saw."

Just Be

OUR DAUGHTER WAS VISITING for the weekend. We had a wonderful, relaxing time, and then she said some words that resonated within me: "This is a place where you can just be."

I agree.

I find time to "just be" in my home, and others have mentioned the peace they experience here.

Isn't that how we are supposed to feel as Christians? Doesn't Jesus want us to "just be" in His presence?

Yes, there is a time for doing. We go to church, study the Bible, visit the sick, go on a mission trip or teach a class. These are all good things.

But there is more.

We need to be doing, but first comes the being.

John 17:21 (MSG)

"Just as you, Father, are in me and I in you, so they might be one heart and mind with us."

Conduit or Crimped?

It was a special weekend away with my husband John and several hundred other motorcycle riders. And I knew just where I wanted to eat in the town of John Day, Oregon—The Outpost.

I ordered my food and an iced tea. The drink came complete with a straw in a clear plastic sheath. Thirsty, I reached for the straw, ripped open the end of the covering, and paused in motion on the way to my glass.

One end of the straw was crimped shut. How was that supposed to work?

As the waitress passed by, I requested a usable straw. I was given one that had an opening on both ends—a useful conduit for my tea. The waitress removed the unusable straw and threw it away.

My mind went into overdrive. When she returned with our food, I asked if she could retrieve the worthless straw for me. It was already in the trash, but she willingly returned it. As we ate, John and I carried on a heavy-duty discussion about that straw.

We know people like that.

As Christ-followers, we are each designed to be a conduit for the good news about God and His love, but some of us have been crimped. Maybe by abusive parents, a legalistic church, or an unfaithful spouse. They've shut off the flow of goodness in their lives and many have been thrown away, worthless.

For thirty years I lay in the trash, crimped and empty.

But worthless straws can be fixed by cutting off the crimped end. That would make it a little shorter than other straws, but still able to be a conduit of liquid from drink to mouth.

Crimped Christ-followers can also be fixed. The length of the straw is not the important part. Long or short, the question is whether you are a channel of blessing allowing God's love to flow through you to others.

Or do you have a crimped end?

Deuteronomy 39:19 (NIV)
"This day I call the heavens and the earth as witnesses against you that I have set before you life and death, blessings and curses."

Green Armbands

EVERYWHERE WE WENT, JOHN and I saw the green armbands. Eating lunch at a restaurant, it was easy to see who was wearing one. Walking around town, we knew immediately if someone had one on. In the grocery store, every other person was sporting a green armband.

Why?

Along with hundreds of other people, we had traveled to John Day, Oregon, to attend a motorcycle rally. You had to register to be allowed through the gate and into the fair grounds where the rally was being held. On registering, a green band was placed on your wrist.

Strangers talked to strangers because they all belonged to the same green band group. We were all in town with a common interest—motorcycles.

Well, almost all. I really didn't care much about the actual motorcycle, but I did care about my husband and friends who rode them.

Isn't that what it's supposed to be like for Christ followers? Wherever we go, can't we find others who belong to Christ? Our common interest allows us freedom to make instant friends when we discover they are a brother or sister in Christ.

The witness of the Holy Spirit is far better than a green armband.

1 Peter 3:8 (NLT)
"Finally, all of you should be of one mind. Sympathize with each other. Love each other as brothers and sisters. Be tenderhearted, and keep a humble attitude."

Good Eye, Bad Eye

MY RIGHT EYE USED to be my bad eye, not functioning properly. In fact, my vision was so blurry I was declared legally blind in that eye. My left eye became the dominant one, taking control of my focus. Then I was given a lens implant in my right eye. Immediately, the vision in that eye was much sharper than my left eye.

My left eye rebelled.

For several years now, my eyes have not worked together. They both want to be in charge, which causes issues such as double vision and slower tracking of movement.

Finally, my optometrist mentioned I had developed a cataract in my left eye. The manifestation of that film over my eye lens resulted in inferior quality of vision.

So, who's in charge now?

As Christ-followers, we face the same issue of *who's in charge*. Sometimes the lines of right and wrong can become blurry. Due to factors in our lives, we may find it difficult to focus. There are forces within us that are at war.

But we are not helpless in this battle. Just as a lens implant restores clear vision, our God can remove the cause of indistinct vision. We don't even have to make an appointment and endure countless tests. He made us and knows us from the inside out. We just need to allow Him to do His work.

1 Corinthians 13:12 (NLT)
"Now we see things imperfectly, like puzzling reflections in a mirror, but then we will see everything with perfect clarity."

Going Through the Motions

IT WAS A BLUSTERY FALL day, with the wind gusting to 35 mph. Leaves swirled down the street as I drove through our neighborhood. Turning right on the main street lined with businesses, I stared in amazement at the man in front of the store to my right. He was busily removing leaves from the parking lot using a leaf blower.

Did he not get it? No matter how hard he worked, he would never make any progress. His actions were futile. Perhaps it was his business and he wanted it to look as good as possible. Maybe he had been hired to clear away the leaves. As long as I could see him in my rearview mirror, he continued going through the motions of blowing away the leaves, a never-ending job.

I've seen Christians like that, and I've been one.

For years I went through the motions of being a Christian. Everyone knew a Christian could be identified by what they wore, words they didn't say, if they carried a Bible, if the ladies wore no makeup or jewelry, and for sure, if they went to church religiously every time there was a service.

Oh yes, I used my religious leaf blower through the wind, rain, sleet, and snow. I would show the world I was a Christian. Little did I know that the world looked at me just like I looked at that man. They probably said, "Does she not get it? Why would I want to go through life just doing the motions?"

My actions were not only futile, but they caused damage in others.

I've put my leaf blower away. I no longer go through the motions. Since I have a personal relationship with Jesus, I am aware of the world around me. If someone has a need and I can help, I show up. Even if that means I miss church.

That's what Jesus would do.

Hebrews 6:1-3

"Anyone who sets himself up as 'religious' by talking a good game is self-deceived. This kind of religion is hot air and only hot air. Real religion, the kind that passes muster before God the Father, is this: Reach out to the homeless and loveless in their plight, and guard against corruption from the godless world."

Gem in the Junk

Do you love to go to yard sales and dig through someone else's junk? What are you looking for? Something that would be a treasure for you?

Or how about the people who use metal detectors? You see them walking around in the park, moving their machines over the ground. Are they looking for junk or do they hope to find some kind of gem?

For years, John and I had a tradition of traveling to Richland to stroll through the annual Arts in the Park. We had been enough years to know that the good stuff is usually on the north end of the park, and the less desirable booths to the south.

One year, as we headed south across the street separating the two sections of the park, John asked if I really wanted to look around down there. He said, "It's usually just junk."

I said, "You never know what you might find in the junk."

Instantly, I had a mental picture of my life. For years, I had been a gem hidden in the junk—I just hadn't known it.

Junk comes in all shapes and sizes. For some, it's alcohol or drugs. Others get lost in the junk of greed. I was covered with the junk of religious oppression, but the junk is not the issue. It's the gem that matters.

Are you covered with junk? God made you to be a gem.

It is painful to be made into a gem. There is grinding involved and cutting off of unnecessary attachments. Some of it is done by God, but there are parts He expects us to do ourselves. It can be very scary. As God has done His work on me, there have been many times I have wanted to give up. But if we want to be a jewel worthy of shining for God, we must go through the refining process.

Do you know you are a gem? Or are you still hidden in junk?

Just as you dig through the tables piled with other people's junk when you go to a yard sale, God is digging through the junk that is covering you, trying to reach the brilliantly shining gem He wants to use.

1 Corinthians 4:7 (NIV)
"But we have this treasure in jars of clay to show that this all-surpassing power is from God ..."

Gathering Storm

WE WATCHED THE CLOUDS building. They darkened and pushed their way into the sky. We sat on our patio designed with an overhanging roof and walls on three sides for just such an occasion as this. If it blew and rained we would still be dry.

The sun was setting and the clouds above us slowly tinted pink. Still no rain or wind, but lightning flashed in the wall of dark clouds.

But we had a solid house, with it's 12-inch thick walls, layers of concrete, Styrofoam, and more concrete. It was built to withstand storms. We knew we could go inside for safety and, knowing that, felt no cause for fear.

My mind returned to my growing up years in Kansas. No way would we have lingered on the porch awaiting the storm. Clouds that looked like that meant danger—hail and tornadoes. For my family, we had no shelter from that raging weather. We lived in two rooms upstairs and the closest shelter was a basement two houses down the street. A gathering storm caused a high level of stress and fear.

Life is like that. Sometimes we see the storm building and coming our way. Where can we go to feel safe? Do we turn to another person, a different job, or move to a new town? Our stress level increases as we consider our puny options.

Or do we turn to the safe and secure shelter under God's wings. There, protected by His mighty power, we feel no fear. He is greater, stronger, and more powerful than any storm life can throw at us.

Psalm 36:7 (NLT)
"How precious is your unfailing love, O God! All humanity finds shelter in the shadow of your wings."

Futility

THE ALARM GOES OFF. Bleary eyed I rise from my bed, dress, exercise, shower, go to work, come home from work, cook dinner, do housework, and go to bed to rise another day and repeat the procedure.

Is there a purpose in this?

Have you ever felt that way?

In my early days, I moved through life as a robot. I'm delighted to tell you I no longer feel that way. I live each day deliberately, focusing on precious present moments and being alert to any contact that could turn into a divine appointment. But the feeling of life being a futile exercise is not new.

In Haggai 1, God is talking to His people:

"Consider how things are going for you. You have planted much but harvested little."

What do you have to show for the long, hard days at work? Or maybe you are exhausted at the end of the day from housework, children, and poor health. Do you feel a lack of reward in those efforts?

"You have food to eat, but not enough to fill you up. You have wine to drink, but not enough to satisfy your thirst."

As an overeater, I certainly understand this one. I have eaten and eaten my way through my days, trying to feel satisfied. Do you search for a food or drink, or something more to satiate your needs?

"You have clothing to wear, but not enough to keep you warm."

Even though you dress in warm clothes, do you still feel cold inside? Or maybe what you wear is just an extension of the mask you don each morning. You long for a warm, fuzzy feeling that is just beyond your reach.

"You earn wages, only to put them in a purse with holes in it."

For years I lived paycheck to paycheck, but there was never enough. My purse had big holes. One day I discovered that God cares about my finances. The Bible gives good counsel on how to handle our money. The bottom line is, don't spend more than you have. It's a simple solution, but not easy to achieve. Only when we turn our money over to Him, will the holes in our purse be mended.

Life is not an exercise in futility. It takes God to help us change our view. When we walk through each day with Him, we see life differently.

Haggai 2:19 (NLT)
"I am giving you a promise now while the seed is still in the barn … But from this day onward I will bless you."

Fitbit

I succumbed to the pressure. All around me I heard comments about the Fitbit and its ability to keep track of how many steps I had taken in a day. I wasn't sure I cared about that, but I was a little curious, since I walk on the treadmill every morning. Apparently, 10,000 steps a day was the goal.

The promo was outstanding regarding what it would do for me. It could help turn my life into a fun path to fitness. I would now know the distance I walked each day and the calories I burned.

Any day, I would be skinny.

But the Fitbit affected me in a different way. If I cared so much about how many steps I took each day, how many miles I walked, and how many calories I consumed to ensure my physical health, then shouldn't I care about my Christian fitness the same way? Where, exactly, was the device that would keep me on track regarding how much I prayed, read my Bible, or just enjoyed quiet time with God?

I still go to the gym first thing in the morning, with my Fitbit hooked to my clothes so I can track my movements. But as I get dressed and reach for it, my mind turns to God, to my blessings, to people who need prayer.

That little device is a constant reminder to me that more than just my physical health is at stake.

Ephesians 4:16 (MSG)
"His very breath and blood flow through us, nourishing us so that we will grow up healthy in God, robust in love."

First Time Mother

SHE SEEMED SO VERY tiny with a darling button nose. I couldn't take my eyes off her. With her fists balled under her chin, her big eyes stared right back. My first child, whose birthday just happens to be today.

It's been quite a journey.

I knew all the basics of childcare. The diapers and bottles, rocking her or walking the floor, singing songs to her, and watching her breathe as she slept. But it takes so much more than that, and no matter how hard you try you can never be that perfect parent. There isn't one.

In the beginning years, I raised her as I had been taught. I crammed religion down her throat and judged her when she failed to live up to my rigid expectations.

Now I am very aware of how misguided I was. She was a teenager before I took a different path, but by then, so many patterns were already ingrained. As I struggled to learn a new way of parenting, one thing didn't change—my love for her.

Now we are adults together and I'm so very proud of her. It's hard to believe how fast those years have flown by. Even though she will always be my daughter, now she is also my friend. We get our nails done and talk at Starbucks. When I go visit her, she is a very gracious hostess and a great tour guide. I've seen everything from Hearst Castle to Westwood in the wee hours of the morning.

Happy birthday to my firstborn.

Psalm 37:26b (NIV)

"... their children will be a blessing."

Expectations

BY DEFINITION, EXPECTATIONS ARE just that: something expected. The media is full of talk about expectations—politics, body and home makeovers, talents.

I'll leave the politics alone, but the body makeover shows give the contestants huge expectations that are unrealistic and unhealthy when talking about results. The young, impressionable audience watching these shows is already self-conscious about their body image. If they buy into these expectations, they are in for a lifetime of unmet expectations and perceived failure, sometimes dying, to achieve that skinny body.

I've watched some of the *American Idol* programs. Contestants fainting, being taken to the hospital and given an IV to hydrate their abused bodies. Being the next *American Idol* is all they live for. If they can just attain that status, life will be forever great.

As I've listened to the politicians, seen videos of young people starving themselves for beauty, and watched the singers, I've thought about expectations, especially when it comes to church.

We all have a set of expectations for our church. Many simply expect the church will always be like Jesus. Are those expectations reasonable, much less Biblical? My church did a study in the book of Acts for 40 days. We found conflict, complaints, dissension, factions, and unmet expectations.

I learned years ago that a church is full of people who are going to act like people. They may disappoint us, hurt us, and tick us off. No church will mesh perfectly with our ideal of what the church is supposed to be.

There is only one Person who can meet all expectations, so we might as well learn how to get along. Exactly why do we go to church anyway?

Psalm 149:1 (MSG)
"Hallelujah! Sing to God a brand-new song; praise Him in the company of all who love Him."

Every End is a New Beginning

Thousands of people were directly affected by what happened that day. Loved ones died. The heroes who helped rescue survivors are now dealing with poor health, damaged just by breathing. On Facebook and emails, in magazines and on television, the question is asked repeatedly. "Where were you when it happened?"

Our memories are still vivid and clear, that moment of unbelief, and then the horrible realization that it was true. Airplanes really had deliberately flown into buildings. Passengers on one airplane really had deliberately caused the plane to crash prematurely so others would be spared.

In the days following the tragedy, the sale of Bibles skyrocketed. We set aside our pettiness. Blacks and whites united. Teenagers and old people hugged. America was united and searching for an answer. But have we found it?

Many things ended that day. Our country lost its naiveté. We became vulnerable. Marriages were suddenly destroyed. Parents and children were gone. For many, financial security no longer existed. Others lost the use of arms, legs, and minds. But every end is a new beginning.

An article in *Time* magazine tells of how life has gone on. Firefighter Jimmy Riches died that day, but his three brothers—Danny, Tommy, and Timmy—joined the NYC Fire Department.

Jeremy Glick lost his life when the plane he was on crashed into a field in Pennsylvania, but his wife is now remarried and they have two children.

I don't know what ended for you that day. Perhaps you had a loved one who was gone in that moment. I didn't, and so your new beginning is much more difficult than mine. But what new beginning have you found?

For me, I found a renewed patriotism, a deeper compassion for heroes, and a greater understanding of just how great God really is.

2 Corinthians 4:16-17 (MSG)

"So we're not giving up. How could we! Even though on the outside it often looks like things are falling apart on us, on the inside, where God is making new life, not a day goes by without his unfolding grace. These hard times are small potatoes compared to the coming good times; the lavish celebration prepared for us."

Escape Ramps

RETURNING HOME FROM A trip to Boise required that I drive on one of the most hazardous stretches of road along westbound Interstate 84, commonly called Cabbage Hill. The road drops about 2,000 feet in six miles with twists and double hairpin turns at a six percent downgrade. Long before I reached the descent, roadside signs appeared to warn me of the upcoming danger and explained about the escape ramps located at Milepost 221 and 220.

Since I've driven that highway many times, I knew what was ahead.

The first escape ramp came into view. I had no need to use it and no one else had plowed into the gravel.

Around a few more turns and there it was: Milepost 220 with a semi embedded in the ramp. Two tow trucks with lights flashing had arrived. Several men were talking beside the stuck truck.

I tried to imagine what it had been like for that driver, picking up speed, barreling around curves, out of control, and searching for the escape ramp.

Life can be like that sometimes. One thing leads to another. Before we know it, life seems out of control. On our wild ride downward, we look frantically for a way out. And then we see it—the escape ramp.

The Bible is full of warning signs telling us of the danger if we continue our wayward lifestyle. And then it explains everything we need to know to stop our dangerous descent.

We just have to read it.

Psalm 119:105-107 (MSG)
"By your words I can see where I'm going; they throw a beam of light on my dark path. Everything's falling apart on me, God; put me together again with your Word."

Eating Oatmeal Always Makes Me Thirsty

LAST NIGHT I ENJOYED a bowl of oatmeal for dinner. Since I try to limit my intake of liquid in the evening to insure a good night's sleep without having to get up, eating oatmeal in the evening was not a good plan.

Eating oatmeal always makes me thirsty. And so, I drank and drank.

A few weeks ago, I met a friend for lunch at a Mexican restaurant. She recently acquired braces and had been instructed to drink no carbonated liquids. She used to have a Pepsi a day, so was suffering from withdrawal. As we visited before the waitress came to take our order, she related her struggle to me.

Eating Mexican food always makes me want a Pepsi.

Yesterday, a close friend who is trying to lose weight shared with me about going to a birthday dinner at a Chinese restaurant. When the meal was over and the fortune cookies were given out, she reached for one and broke it in two, ready to pop half in her mouth. That's when she remembered she had sworn off sweets, so placed the cookie on her plate. Her comment was, "It's amazing how much we eat by rote."

Eating Chinese food is always accompanied with a fortune cookie.

How many other areas of our lives are made to conform to cravings or habit? As I've pondered that question through this day, I'm very aware of many of mine.

What are you doing by rote?

1 Corinthians 7:24 (MSG)
"So please don't, out of old habit, slip back into being or doing what everyone else tells you."

Famine

THE PICTURES BROUGHT A stab of pain to my heart—little children and babies starving to death in Somalia, their mothers with anguish on their faces. Some had been walking for a month trying to find help and had lost a child or more to death on the way.

As the news and images continued, my thoughts were scattered. *How awful. Those people live in the same world I do. Why them and not me? How do those mothers take it? What can I do?*

This morning, I could not get those pictures out of my mind. I live such a blessed life. I've been hungry a few times in my life, but never starving; never emaciated and lifeless.

That's when my mind turned to a different kind of famine. The starving people shown on the news are on the other side of the world. But we are experiencing a famine in our own land—in our United States—that isn't being talked about on the nightly news. Those starving people do not look emaciated. They are executives, sports people, movie stars, the neighbor next door. Sometimes they commit suicide. Others die of drug and alcohol abuse.

Just as you and I want to be loved and accepted, so do they. Some have traveled a long way seeking assistance, but in the world they live, the right kind of help is not available.

Once again, I think, *How awful. Those people live in the same world I do. What can I do?*

I am very aware that I come in contact with starving people every day—starving for love and acceptance.

I would gladly share my food with the starving children in Somalia, but I need to be willing to give love and acceptance to the people in my own world. I need to help them discover hope by introducing them to the unfailing source—Jesus.

John 6:35 (NLT)
"Jesus replied, 'I am the bread of life. Whoever comes to me will never be hungry again. Whoever believes in me will never be thirsty.'"

Extremes

YEARS AGO, WHEN I was younger, I rode on the back of John's motorcycle when he took trips. The very first one introduced me to the extreme heat of Hell's Canyon in July. The name should have been a clue. As I moved into a zombie state I wondered how well John was holding up. I was the hottest I have ever been, at least for an extended period of time. I just wanted off.

Months later, John shared the coldest ride with me. We traveled to a nearby town (about 30 miles away) and spent the evening. When it was time to return home, the temperature had dropped to 40 degrees. We had no heated gear, just jeans, our coats and helmets. Exactly what is the wind chill factor when it's 40 degrees and you are moving at 60 MPH? I don't know, but nothing functioned when it was time to climb off the bike. My hands wouldn't let go and my legs were unable to straighten. I just fell off the bike.

There are people who call themselves Christians, but are far from it. The Westboro Baptist Church in Topeka, Kansas, is one such group. By their own count, they have conducted over 30,000 pickets at funerals, in all 50 states, at an estimated cost of $250,000. To them, everyone is fair game.

They are an extreme religious "hate" group. Ironic, isn't it?

There are other churches that really have no belief in Jesus. They just want you to feel good. As long as you try to be nice, then it's all good. Here are some snippets from one such church:

Their master is a guiding spirit and the holy book is a sacred manuscript of nature. Their religion is the unswerving progress in the right direction. They follow the law of reciprocity, which is observed by a selfless conscience … and it goes on.

I am so grateful I was able to break away from an extreme church.

Psalm 19:12-13

"But what happens when we live God's way? He brings gifts into our lives, much the same way that fruit appears in an orchard—things like affection for others, exuberance about life, serenity … We find ourselves involved in loyal commitments, not needing to force our way in life, able to marshal and direct our energies wisely."

Duty Fulfilled

MY FIRST CAR WAS a little Datsun. Not much of a car, but it got me from here to there. I've since had Honda Accords and Civics. They were nicer than the Datsun, had a little more power, and got me from here to there. My Maxima was nice. I liked the color and the roominess. But its duty was to get me from here to there.

Then I came up in the world. I looked for a car I actually wanted, not just a service vehicle. An Acura TL was my car of choice. Nice. Had some power. But it still got me from here to there.

Now I own a Hyundai Sonata. Turbo Charged. And it gets me from here to there. Sometimes faster.

Then I was given the opportunity to ride in a Corvette. Six gears. Over 500 HP. A variety of options and buttons. I experienced going from zero to 100 MPH in seconds. My head whipped and the tires chattered. I grinned.

But it still just got us from here to there.

There are all kinds of Christ-followers. Some are quiet and stay behind the scenes, sending cards of encouragement and taking time to pray for people. Others are more active, volunteering at church, working at the mission, and taking someone to lunch. Then there are the Christ-followers who travel the world sharing the Gospel. Their names are familiar to many.

But bottom line, we are all just fulfilling the duty we were designed for.

Philippians 2:14-15 (MSG)
"Do everything readily and cheerfully—no bickering, no second-guessing allowed! Go out into the world uncorrupted, a breath of fresh air in this squalid and polluted society. Provide people with a glimpse of good living and of the living God. Carry the light-giving Message into the night ..."

Dull of Hearing

LISTENING TO CHUCK SWINDOLL's podcast, I couldn't get past a phrase he used: *dull of hearing.* Think about it a minute. How many people do you know who are dull of hearing?

Children are very good at this. You ask them to do something, and nothing happens. You ask again. Still nothing. I've watched, time and again, as parents resort to yelling to get a child's attention. Is the child dull of hearing, or have they just trained the parent how to react?

It doesn't get better when they are teenagers. With loud music plugged into their ears, they may very well be dull of hearing. But teenagers also live in their own world and tune others out.

Now to the nitty-gritty. How about spouses? Are any of you dull of hearing? Does your spouse have to throw things, yell, cry, or leave to get your attention?

To be dull of hearing can apply to any type of relationship, including my relationship with God. His book tells me the way He wants me to live. If I choose to be dull of hearing, I will ignore the words of wisdom and go my own way.

In the same way that there are consequences for the child who doesn't listen, or the spouse who seems not to hear, I reap the consequences of not listening to God. It may take years before I finally hear what He has been saying all along.

Matthew 17:5 (NASB)

"While He was still speaking, a bright cloud overshadowed them, and behold, a voice out of the cloud said, "This is My beloved Son, with whom I am well-pleased; listen to Him."

Dropping the Needle

I LEARNED TO KNIT using circular needles. As I worked my way across the row and reached the end, I would let go of the empty needle, turn the work around, and begin the next row. That process functioned just fine until I started a project that called for straight knitting needles.

No problem.

I worked my way across the row, reached the end, and promptly dropped my knitting needle on the floor. *Oops.* I had forgotten I wasn't using a circular needle. I picked up the fallen needle, turned the project around, worked my way across the row, and dropped my knitting needle on the floor.

Slow learner.

After a few times of watching me bend over and pick up the needle, my husband could take it no longer. "What are you doing?"

Even though I knew the real question, I answered, "Knitting."

His curiosity was not satisfied with that response. So I had to admit I had a very short memory and that my programming using a circular needle was causing issues.

I find I have the same issues in life.

It's hard to re-program when you've spent a lifetime of unhealthy eating. The healthy food makes it to your mouth for a day or two, and then the bad eating habits kick in.

Or maybe you've been trained to say "yes" to anything asked of you, even though you are already stressed. When you decide to take charge of your time, to learn to say "no", you still find the words, "Sure, I'll do that" coming out of your mouth.

And the hardest reprogramming for me was to undo my legalistic, religious training. Even though I was striving to be non-judgmental, the words that spewed from my mouth were harsh and condemnatory.

I'm still working on that one, but as least I haven't dropped any needles lately.

1 Corinthians 4:5 (NLT)
"So don't make judgments about anyone ahead of time—before the Lord returns. For he will bring our darkest secrets to light and will reveal our private motives. Then God will give to each one whatever praise is due."

Dressed for Work

AS I SAT AT THE computer at seven in the morning, I thought of how I was dressed. The store where I worked did not open until eight. It was my day off, but due to the absence of others, I felt I could help out by dropping by and doing the morning bookkeeping duties.

The software program did not care I was dressed in my exercise clothes and wore a baseball cap. All it needed was for me to push the right buttons on the keyboard.

I've been to churches where how you dressed was the criteria for being a "Christian". If you weren't dressed the part, God could not use you.

God looks on the inside. All He asks is that we "push" the right keys. Love others. Help feed, clothe, and shelter them. Be His hands. Listen to people. Let Him be the judge.

Are you dressed for work? Or are you a living extension of Him wherever you go?

2 Corinthians 5:12b (NASB)

"... so that you will have an answer for those who take pride in appearance and not in heart."

Dirty Hands

WHEN MY KIDS WERE little, after a day of playing outside, I would tell them to wash their hands before dinner. From the bathroom would come sounds of water running and various conversations.

"You didn't wash your hands good enough. There's still dirt right there."

"I got my hands washed first. You're just slow."

"Your hands are clean enough. A little dirt is okay."

Competitions. Comparisons.

Isn't the same true in life? There's always someone who will tell you exactly where your dirt is. Or maybe they take life as a competition and they want to finish first. Others are quite willing to keep a little dirt. It won't hurt anybody.

As a Christ-follower, I want to be careful about that kind of behavior. Even though I have washed my life with God's love, it's not my job to tell someone else where their dirt is. They are all too aware of the issues in their life that are dragging them down. Nor should I go around expressing pride in my status as a Christ-follower.

Then there are those who want to get by with as little Christianity as possible—just enough to make it to heaven, but not interfere in their earthly passions. My heart goes out to them for the empty life they lead.

Jesus is in the hand-washing business. No competitions. No comparisons. Just clean.

1 Corinthians 6:11 (MSG)
"Since then, you've been cleaned up and given a fresh start by Jesus."

Digging in God's Dirt

IT HAPPENED AGAIN. I learned a lesson about God from my dog.

We've had Charlie, our dog, since 2011, and he's never been a digger. So imagine my surprise when we returned home from church one Sunday to discover the contents from one of my planters on the patio, spread around like decorations on the concrete.

My investigation of the damage showed some of the plants no longer had roots. Had Charlie suddenly become a vegetarian?

Even though he was disciplined, we had to remember that Charlie is, after all, a dog. Those were my thoughts as I tried to salvage the uprooted plants. The pot still needed some work. It was only two-thirds full, but it could be restored with the purchase of more flowers.

Rising from my knees, I noticed that the water in Charlie's dish was dirty and almost empty. I cleaned it out and gave him fresh water. That's when it hit me. As a human being, trying to follow Christ, I mess with God's plan. I dig in His dirt and uproot what He has designed. I leave a trail of damage.

After all, I am human.

But God cleans up my messes and even gives me fresh water for my soul. He surveys the two-thirds full pot and restores it to fullness, filling it with beauty and life.

Have you been digging in His dirt lately?

John 6:63 (NLT)

"Human effort accomplishes nothing."

Crash Dump

IT HAPPENED AGAIN. THE blue screen of death; crash dump.

I try to live a good life, be a nice person and treat my computer right. Yet I've now seen the blue screen of death on at least five different computers. My heart does a little lurch when I see the words "crash dump."

The first one took me totally by surprise. I lost everything. I began to rely heavily on advice from our computer technician. He scheduled backups to a disk so if the blue screen happened again I would still have my information.

Sure enough, it did, but I had no worries. I had my backup disk.

But guess what? The new computer could not restore from the disk. It was unreadable. All was lost again.

In the years since then, I have learned about backups and external hard drives and cloud storage. All information I never wanted to have to learn.

Isn't life like that?

We never know when the blue screen of death may occur. We live our lives being nice and treating people right. Then, one day, we experience a crash dump. My first one occurred with the word "divorce."

I began to rely heavily on Someone who knew all about crash dumps. I turned to Him again and again, learning all about His restoration program that never has a glitch.

As long as He is my backup, I never have to worry about that blue screen of death. I have the perfect cloud storage—heaven.

Matthew 13:11 (NIV)
"He replied, 'Because the knowledge of the secrets of the kingdom of heaven has been given to you ...'"

Counting the Chimes

IN THE QUIET OF the house, I counted the chimes the clock sounded out—seven times. Yet I knew I had begun ironing at 1:30, probably 30 minutes ago. The knowledge that our wonderful timepiece no longer worked correctly gave me pause. The clock had been a gift from God in the form of a tax refund.

Years before, John and I had spotted it at Costco—the only one. We agreed we both liked it, which was unusual, but the purchase just wasn't in our budget.

On the way home from the store, our accountant called to tell us the good news about our income tax. The refund amount exactly covered the price.

We did a U-turn.

Over the years, I've counted on that clock. Wherever I was in my home, I knew what time it was without looking. Especially in the night, when I didn't want to disturb John, I would lay in the dark counting the chimes to see if it was close enough to morning to get up.

Now I could no longer count on it.

I thought of people who have crossed my path, become someone I could count on, solid in their faith and wisdom. Yet something happened to cause them to become unreliable.

My thoughts turned to me. Have I been that person? When I speak forth, can others count on me?

Can they count on you?

Romans 1:21-22 (MSG)
"People knew God perfectly well, but when they didn't treat him like God, refusing to worship him, they trivialized themselves into silliness and confusion so that there was neither sense nor direction left in their lives. They pretended to know it all, but were illiterate regarding life."

Click on the Save Button

WITH THE ADVENT OF computers, common words with new meanings have entered our vocabulary. One with which I am very familiar is the *save* button. When I am writing an article or blog, I click *save* regularly. That's why my attention was caught by the T-shirt with the picture of earth, a save button, and a hand ready to click on the button. I bought it and am wearing it as I type.

Our earth is in dire need of saving.

According to the World Hunger Education Service, there were 925 million hungry people in the world in 2010. I can't even wrap my mind around that many starving and malnourished people. On top of that, we have been besieged with flooding, hurricanes, tornadoes, earthquakes, tsunamis, and out of control fires. Countries are being overthrown, economic crisis is rampant and over one million people die by suicide worldwide each year (International Suicide Statistics).

It's time to click on that *save* button now.

But as a Christ-follower, I see another meaning for the word *save.* Missionaries travel around the world to spread the good news about Jesus. Ministers stand behind pulpits on Sunday morning, declaring God's love for a hurting world. But it takes more than that. One individual, living a life of integrity and following the precepts of Jesus speaks volumes to the people in their world.

Our earth is in dire need of saving, and that endeavor starts with you and me.

Romans 10:14-15 (MSG)
"But how can people call for help if they don't know who to trust? And how can they know who to trust if they haven't heard of the One who can be trusted? And how can they hear if nobody tells them?"

Checking the Rearview Mirror

SEVERAL YEARS AGO, I was rear-ended as I waited to turn left into our home street. There were no cars behind me when I stopped, but checking in my rearview mirror, I could see one coming several blocks back. That car never even slowed down.

Now I have trouble sitting on a street, waiting to turn left. I am checking my rearview mirror as much as I am watching the traffic going the other way.

Sometimes life is like that.

We've been hurt in the past, so we spend as much time looking at the past as we do looking to the future. The chances of another car deciding to just run into me from the rear are rather slim (I'm counting on that). And if we learn from past hurts and don't allow ourselves to get in those situations, the chances are slim we will be hurt like that again.

The future stretches out before us.

Are you living life looking in your rearview mirror?

Philippians 3:13b-14a (NIV)
"Forgetting what lies behind and straining torward what is ahead, I press on ..."

Check Again

LUNCH WAS OVER, AND John and I headed back to the parking lot. As we came within a few feet of my car, I noticed something wasn't quite right. The license plate was a Boise number.

It wasn't my car.

Two cars, same parking lot, same make and color, but oh, so different.

When I walked around to the right side of the Boise car, it was discolored from repair work after a wreck.

Definitely not my car.

But looks can be deceiving. You can be in a relationship with someone who gives off all the right signals, says all the right things, but they are wearing a mask. When you get close enough, you discover the damage from a previous divorce.

Or maybe you think you've finally found the perfect job. A few months in, you begin to understand that you didn't ask the right questions. Your employer expects things from you that require too much overtime, or maybe they put the pressure on for you to look the other way while some illegal activities take place.

Pastors are not immune to mask wearing. Some churches place their pastor on a pedestal. He can do no wrong as he leads his flock down a treacherous path. A combination of charisma and cunning can make it very difficult to see that something is just not right.

Before you climb in the wrong car, check again.

Ephesians 5:15 (AMP)
"Look carefully then how you walk! Live purposefully and worthily and accurately, not as the unwise and witless, but as wise (sensible, intelligent people)."

Change of Address

BEFORE I WAS OLD enough to understand about addresses, I lived at 118 South Rural. From there we moved to 22 West Street, 714 Cottonwood, and then 723 Sunnyslope. By then I had entered my teen years. I married and had many addresses during that union, starting with three different abodes in Bethany, Oklahoma.

In rapid succession we moved from Oklahoma to Kansas, where we moved four times, then on to Texas and back to Oklahoma. From there the moving van hauled our possessions to North Carolina, Maryland, and back to Oklahoma, where we had two different addresses. The final move in that marriage was to Nebraska, involving three different houses.

By then I had reached the ripe old age of 30.

I've moved another ten times. My last change of address was into a new home with my husband John. As I thought about this wonderful new home, built specifically for John and me, designed to see us into old age, I realized this is not my last address.

I will have at least one more—heaven.

Viewing this home from that perspective makes all the difference in this world. Yes, it's a beautiful, solid, energy-efficient home. We live comfortably within its walls, but it is not our final home, it's just ours to enjoy for now.

It's a temporary address, and so is yours.

Postscript: This was written before John's death. He now lives in heaven.

Hebrews 11:14-16 (msg)

"They saw it way off in the distance, waved their greeting, and accepted the fact that they were transients in this world. People who live this way make it plain that they are looking for their true home. If they were homesick for the old country, they could have gone back any time they wanted. But they were after a far better country than that—heaven country."

Buckled In

I WAS ONLY GOING a few blocks down a side street. As I started to buckle my seat belt, I stopped just short of inserting it in the clasp. I held the V of the strap in my thumb near the clasp for the short trip. I figured if I passed a policeman it would look like I had my seatbelt secured.

What would have happened if I had been in a wreck? I'm sure holding the strap in my hand would have done little to keep me from being injured or perhaps killed.

That got me thinking of some people who go to church on Sunday with their Bibles in hand.

How many of them go to church to "look good," meet other nice people, or perhaps even feel they have done the right thing like their parents told them to do? I did that for a number of years.

Until they have inserted their lives into the solid clasp of Jesus Christ as their Savior and King, they are in danger of an inevitable crash that will separate them from eternal life in heaven.

Matthew 7:22-23 (MSG)

"I can see it now—at the Final Judgment thousands strutting up to me and saying, 'Master, we preached the Message, we bashed the demons, our God-sponsored projects had everyone talking.' And do you know what I am going to say? 'You missed the boat. All you did was use me to make yourselves important. You don't impress me one bit. You're out of here.'"

Broken Pieces

IT WAS AN ACCIDENT. Suddenly, with a swipe of John's hand up the side of my face, the right earpiece on my glasses snapped in two. I felt the broken piece fall down my cheek.

"It's broken."

"No, it can't be. I didn't bump it that hard."

Yet, there lay the worthless earpiece holding up nothing.

But no problem. Anyone who needs glasses to make it through the day always has a backup pair. I reached in my drawer, pulled out the glasses case, opened it and removed a mirror image of my broken glasses.

The left earpiece was missing.

After my laughter subsided, I pondered what to do. If I could find an optical shop open on Saturday, they could remove the right earpiece from my backup pair and attach it where my missing right earpiece belonged. I called a local store and explained the situation.

"No problem. Just bring both pair in and we can fix it for you."

I entered the shop, handed both glasses to the technician, and was told, "Oh, sorry, we don't work on that brand. You'll have to go to the shop where you bought them."

That meant waiting until Monday.

Isn't life just like that?

Suddenly a piece of your life is missing. Maybe divorce caused the empty spot. I see the advertisements of organizations offering a place to look for your backup—other people who have a piece missing.

But I have a better idea. Go to the Person who made you. He offers wholeness, even though you feel damaged.

Colossians 1:20 (MSG)

"... all the broken and dislocated pieces of the universe—people and things, animals and atoms—get properly fixed and fit together in vibrant harmonies ..."

Boise State

I'm a Boise State football fan ... or maybe I should say was. Kellen and his peers have graduated and moved on. At one of their games, I purchased an orange and blue baseball cap that said *Broncos* and had a picture of a horse's head on the front. The little strap across the back said *Boise State*.

Yet, repeatedly, people said to me, "Go Broncos. I love Denver."

A little miffed that they would mistake Boise for Denver, I researched the colors and logo for Denver. Guess what? The website was orange and blue and had a horse's head.

My husband presented me with a T-shirt that says *Boise State* on it. No more confusion about where my loyalties lie. In the grocery store and at the gym, wherever I wear my T-shirt, people comment on their love for Boise State.

I wonder, as I go through my day, what am I telling others about my faith? Does carrying my Bible declare me a Christ-follower? I don't take it in the grocery store or to the gym. Do my words, or even my facial expressions, tell others I am a fan of Christ? Just as the Denver Broncos and Boise State have the same colors and logo, so there are many religions that look the same.

My T-shirt clearly states I'm a Boise State fan. So I ponder exactly how to make it clear to those around me that I love Christ.

Philippians 2:14-15 (MSG)
"Do everything readily and cheerfully—no bickering, no second-guessing allowed! Go out into the world uncorrupted, a breath of fresh air in this squalid and polluted society. Provide people with a glimpse of good living and of the living God."

Blinking Lessons

My eyes had been very dry. When I awoke, my first action was to place a finger on my eyelid and lift up, unsticking it from my eyeball. At least my eye was open, but I was still not seeing clearly. Then I would put one drop in each eye, blink a few times and my world showed up. I could see.

It was recommended I attend a Dry Eye Clinic. For two hours I was tested with various machines and instruments. As I placed my chin on the indicated cup, I looked through to a screen. The technician continued to make adjustments to the machine, so we kept talking.

"Ok, that's all for that test. You can set back."

What test?

Pictures had been taken of my blinking. Guess what? When I blinked, my eyelid did not go all the way down to the bottom lid. That is where the moisture resides for your eyeball. I had already been tested to see if I actually had moisture in the tubes. I did. But because I did not blink all the way down, the liquid to moisten my eye stayed in the tube. Thus, my dry eyes.

She asked me to blink. Easy, right?

Wrong. My eyelid action was called partial blinking. I was given a course in blinking exercises, to be completed as a regular part of my day. I now know how to blink correctly. My eyes have improved dramatically.

But I have a question. How many activities in life are completed by rote with no idea we are doing them incorrectly. Who knew I didn't know how to blink? How about the task of studying? Not all children learn the same way. Is it possible the child who struggles needs to learn a new way of studying? What about the way we show love to our spouse? My husband and I had to learn what spoke love to the other.

Then there is the subject of Christianity. Is the way we "do God" working? Maybe we need some God lessons.

Philippians 3:15 (msg)
"So let's keep focused on that goal, those of us who want everything God has for us. If any of you have something else in mind, something less than total commitment, God will clear your blurred vision—you'll see it yet!"

Are You Listening to the Real Song

THE STRAINS OF THE song *Autumn Leaves* filled the air. I reached for my iPhone, wondering what alarm was going off. You see, on iPhones, you can use songs for the alarm. I stared at the screen of the phone.

That particular alarm was not sounding.

My iPad was playing music from my iTunes selection. The song next in the shuffle had been the real *Autumn Leaves*.

I had confused the two.

Don't we do that in life? I think of the brochure I received in the mail this week, advertising a local church. As I read the words, it sounded like a real church. But I've talked with people who believed the advertising and attended. They didn't go back when it was made clear you didn't have to believe in Jesus to be a Christian.

It wasn't a real church.

It is confusing when the words sound so great. We have churches that actually fall under the category of cults. I grew up in one. It takes so much more than a building and a pastor to be real.

Are you listening to the real song?

1 Thessalonians 5:19-21 (MSG)

"Don't suppress the Spirit, and don't stifle those who have a word from the Master. On the other hand, don't be gullible. Check out everything, and keep only what's good."

All Seeing Sensor

A PHENOMENON OCCURRED AT the grocery store this morning, and that doesn't happen often. I needed something in the frozen food section. I turned my grocery cart into the darkened aisle and suddenly the first frozen food case on each side of me was illuminated. When my cart moved further into the aisle, the next two cases lit up.

It was amazing, like someone was watching me and giving me light when I needed it.

I know. I know. Somewhere there was a sensor. But as I continued shopping, my thoughts returned to that aisle.

As a Christ-follower, we have an all-seeing Sensor. Sometimes the way seems really dark as we step into the test being given us and we can't see ahead. But all that is required of us is that we just take that next step. When illumination is needed, it will be provided.

Every time.

Psalm 119:105 (MSG)
"By your words I can see where I'm going; they throw a beam of light on my dark path,"

Adjustments

I LEFT THE HAIR salon with the thought in mind that I would stop by the cleaners on the way home to get that errand out of the way. But there was nothing ready at the cleaners.

I adjusted.

Heading down the street toward home, I could see the dreaded orange "road work" signs. As I got closer, I read "traffic revision ahead." Not wanting to deal with that, I turned right to go over to the next street. After a few blocks, I turned left to head home. Guess what? Road work signs ahead.

I adjusted again.

But now I was passing by the gas station, so I might as well buy my gas and mark another thing off my to do list. Traffic cones blocked the pumps that would allow me to have the gas tank on the correct side.

More adjusting.

I had to drive all the way around and come at the pumps from the other direction. I opened my gas tank, slid the credit card in the slot, lifted the gas hose from the holder and placed it in the tank. The screen said, "begin fueling," but when I squeezed on the handle, no gas was flowing. After repeatedly attempting to achieve fueling, I asked for help.

Again, with the adjustments.

A panel was removed from the backside of the pump, mysterious movements were seen, and then my knight in shining armor arrived. The whole process had to be repeated with the credit card and lifting the handle, but this time it worked.

As I drove home, I re-lived the last few minutes. That's exactly how life is.

Maybe you had plans to go to college, but then your mom lost her job and you had some adjustments to make. Or perhaps that marriage made in heaven didn't work out after all. That certainly calls for traffic revisions ahead. And then there is the issue of squeezing the handle for the purpose of getting gas. Sometimes we can squeeze all we want, but the desired result just doesn't happen.

How good are you at adjustments?

Proverbs 15:15 (MSG)
"A miserable heart means a miserable life; a cheerful heart fills the day with song."

Accustomed to the Darkness

I AVOID THE INTAKE of caffeine. Yet, on a recent road trip, I indulged at Starbucks in the morning with chai. I partook of Mexican food at a restaurant about three in the afternoon. I can't eat Mexican without pop, so I also ordered a Diet Pepsi. And then a refill.

I should have known better.

We arrived home that evening, and for the first hour after we went to bed, I lay there wide-eyed, staring into the dark. Enough of that.

I snuck from the bedroom, feeling my way to the door. Traversing the living room, I discovered the suitcases were still there after tripping over them.

Finally I arrived at my office and turned on the light. A blog was written.

Time to try the bed again, but this time I went through the kitchen to avoid the suitcases. Even though I had turned the lights off when I left my office, I paused at the bedroom door. *I need to let my eyes get accustomed to the darkness so I can make my way to the bed.*

I stood there until I began to see shapes in the dark, and then I entered the bedroom and went to bed.

As I thought about that experience, I realized that life could happen just like that. We spend time in the light doing good things, having high integrity and great morals. But something occurs to cause us to be in darkness, feeling our way. If we stay in that darkness long enough, it becomes familiar. We can find our way around without the light.

It's easier to get away with bad behavior in the dark. Some people like it there and choose to stay.

For me, as a Christ-follower, I choose the Light.

Luke 11:36 (NLT)

"Make sure the light you think you have is not really darkness. If you are filled with light, with no dark corners, then your whole life will be radiant, as though a floodlight is shining on you."

A Slap in the Face

It's been in the news lately, complete with a picture of the New York Police Officer kneeling down beside a homeless man. The officer purchased some boots for the shoeless man, to help keep his feet warm. A visitor from out of state took the photo and it went viral with the viewers blessing the police officer for his kindness.

Yet the latest news is the homeless man is shoeless again. He's hidden his boots somewhere safe because they are worth a lot. And he wants compensation from the photographer for his picture going around the world.

That's like a slap in the face of the kind police officer.

I've been slapped like that before, going out of my way to provide "care" packages for someone who says, "If you think giving me stuff like that and a gift card makes you a good person who are soooo wrong." Or the time I purchased a coat for someone, like the police officer, wanting to help them be warm, and they took it back for the money.

A slap in the face of kindness.

But as I've thought about that homeless man's actions, I couldn't help but wonder how many times I've slapped God in the face. In His mercy, He provides something I need. But in my arrogance or ignorance, I reject that offer for something of my own choosing.

Have you slapped anyone lately?

Proverbs 1:23-24 (MSG)

"About face! I can revise your life. Look, I'm ready to pour out my spirit on you; I'm ready to tell you all I know. As it is, I've called, but you've turned a deaf ear; I've reached out to you, but you've ignored me."

A New Way of Typing

THE OBJECT WAS TO push down hard on the keys, causing the chosen font to strike the paper and spell the word correctly. If you hit an incorrect key, then more time was taken to use Liquid Paper, which you brushed over the incorrect letter, allowed it to dry, and then hit the correct key.

If you wanted a capital letter, that involved locking down a separate key. And when you reached the end of each line, your left hand reached for the lever to push the carriage to the right to begin the next line, rolling the platen down one row at the same time. When the ribbon became so worn you could hardly see the print on the page, then you had to change it.

It's called a manual typewriter.

After typing this way for years, I had to learn to type on a computer keyboard for my job. When I first began using the computer keyboard, I pushed very forcefully on the keys. There was no need for that. A mere finger stroke produced a letter on the screen. And if I hit the wrong key and spelled the word incorrectly, all I had to do was backspace and, *poof*, the mistake was gone. No more correction liquid was needed. There were no levers to push and no need to change ribbon.

There are people who have been dealing with life like it's a manual typewriter. It's all they've ever known and so they push hard on the other person. If they don't get the desired results, they think yelling will bring about a correction. Sometimes they actually use their hands to make the changes they want. Other times they just change ribbons.

Know anyone like that?

It is possible for them to learn to deal with others using a different approach. But first they have to feel the need to make such a scary change and lose the only control they think they have. There will be trial and error in the learning process. It will take someone—spouse, friend, counselor, or pastor—with discernment to be willing to help them learn a new way of "typing."

Are you available?

Romans 12:2 (NLT)
"Don't copy the behavior and customs of this world, but let God transform you into a new person by changing the way you think ..."

A Life of Integrity

Chuck Swindoll has a series of podcasts about Daniel. I've heard the story of Daniel my whole life, yet Chuck brought out a point new to me. But before we get to that, first, the lion's den.

Daniel was not thrown into the lion's den because he did something wrong, but due to his unswerving belief in God. He made others in power nervous. So they investigated Daniel's life, searching for an illegal transaction here or a secret addiction there.

They could find nothing.

They trapped him by instigating a decree that he bow down and worship someone other than the real God. If he were caught praying to his God, he would be killed. Yet Daniel continued his daily practice of kneeling by an open window and pouring out his heart in prayer three times a day.

His spies caught him, took him to the king, and arrangements were made for him to be thrown into a den of hungry lions.

Here's the information I had never heard before. Daniel was 80 years old when this took place!

My ponderings turned to my own life. If I had spies watching me, what would they find? Am I living a life of high integrity or just mediocrity? Would I be willing to continue my worship of God so openly if I knew it meant my death?

What about you?

Proverbs 10:9 (NIV)

"Whoever walks in integrity walks securely, but whoever takes crooked paths will be found out."

A Difference in Price

RESERVATIONS HAD BEEN MADE. Airline tickets purchased. We were going on a big adventure and I really wished we had better luggage. We had traveled many miles with our old luggage. It was bulky and very old school. The wheels didn't even spin. Due to some health issues, I thought it would be helpful if we could have lighter, more maneuverable suitcases.

I pushed that thought to the back of my mind as I ran my errands.

It was when I stopped to pick up some prescriptions that I saw a sale for luggage—half price. I skidded to a stop. Really? American Tourister. The tag said, "light weight." I reached for the 25-inch suitcase. Easy peasy. And it had spinner wheels. On the shelf above it was a 21-inch case. They were the last of the blue ones.

It was no easy task to place them in the cart, and then without being able to see where I was going, I pushed the cart blindly through the aisles to the check out. The young man scanned the smaller one first, a few more of my items, and then came the second suitcase.

"Are these alike?"

They were both American Tourister, so I nodded, but as I walked to the car, a thought niggled in the back of my mind. *What did he mean by that question? What if he thought the second suitcase was the same size as the first one? He would have charged me the same price for both of them.*

Out of the blue came the thought, *If I don't look at the receipt, I'll never know if I got the larger one for the price of the smaller.*

Just as quickly, shame filled me. Did I want to be able to sleep with a clear conscience? I looked at the receipt.

It was a hassle and time-consuming to get back in line and make the correction in price. No one thanked me for my honesty. They did complain about the difficulty in figuring it out since I also had used a discount coupon. But it was about so much more than a price tag on a piece of luggage. I would have paid a huge difference in the price if I had been dishonest.

I smiled as I walked out.

Proverbs 10:9 (NLT)
"People with integrity walk safely, but those who follow crooked paths will slip and fall."

Distractions

THE TREADMILL I USE every morning at the gym faces out a window. When I stepped up on the track today, I noticed a police car sitting across the street in the church parking lot. *Aha!* He was looking for speeders. He was at the ending edge of a school zone. Cars coming past him would have been notified earlier to slow to 20 MPH.

Yet, even with that warning, they did not slow down. In a matter of minutes, three of them had been pulled over with the dreaded flashing lights behind them.

And then the policeman gave one more ticket. I watched as he took off toward the school zone, lights flashing.

You've got to be kidding.

Any car headed toward the zone could easily see the police car sitting there and the blinking yellow light saying 20 MPH. Apparently, slowing down for this car was not an option as it cruised past the police.

As I pondered how very stupid that was, I remembered something from the previous week. I had been busy writing a blog in my head and cruised right past the street I planned to turn down. Was that stupid? I believe it's called distracted driving.

Life is just like that. It's call distracted living.

What is it that distracts you? Worry? Stress? Compulsions? We can get so caught up in our own drama that we miss the signs that tell us there is trouble in our family, our job, or with our friends. Then we are shocked when a child leaves home too soon, a divorce splits friends, or a co-worker is no longer around.

I'm going to try to not write while I drive. What choice will you make?

Proverbs 4:25 (MSG)
"Keep your eyes straight ahead; ignore all sideshow distractions."

The Grass is Not Always Greener

I STOOD IN LINE at the bank behind a short lady, about the same height as me. In front of her was a very tall young man. I listened in on their conversation.

"So, do you play basketball?"

"No, I'm an IT consultant."

"But you probably played basketball when you were younger. Right?"

"No, I've never played basketball."

"I wish I was tall. It's so difficult to be this short. I have to ask for help at the grocery store to get items off the top shelf. There are so many things around the house I can't accomplish because I'm so short. It must be great to be that tall. How tall are you?

"Six foot ten.

"Oh my. That's *really* tall."

"Well it has a whole set of issues I will have to deal with the rest of my life. Most chairs don't fit me. I have to duck through every door. It's hard to find clothes for me. And being this tall comes with back problems. I don't know how long I can keep working. My back is too painful, and I'm only 26 years old."

It was his turn to be waited on, so the conversation ceased, but my spinning mind did not. How often we see others as having advantages over us. We do a lot of "if only" in our head. We have no idea what the other person is dealing with.

Grass is not always greener on the other side.

Luke 18:14b (MSG)

"... but if you're content to be simply yourself, you will become more than yourself."

Set Apart

I GREW UP IN a church that believed the Bible when it told us to be "set apart." That meant we were to have nothing to do with anyone who didn't attend our church. I know other denominations and religious sects that feel the same way.

I was always set apart at school and in my neighborhood. If I got too close to others, their worldliness might rub off on me.

I wondered about the scriptures that spoke of Christians being the light in the darkness and the salt of the earth. How, exactly, could we do that if we kept ourselves separate?

Today, the world I live in has gone nuts. As I watch the news and read the newspapers, I am so grateful for the peace within me. As a Christ-follower I know the end result. I feel like I'm an observer, watching the craziness from the outside.

And then it hit me. I *am* set apart.

But I don't have to live an isolated life, making sure to have no contact with someone who does not believe as I do. That's good, because I have many of those.

I am set apart because of my belief in Jesus. What the culture of this current world does cannot separate me from Him. I can calmly look on from the sidelines, pray, and be grateful for my peace.

Leviticus 20:26 (NASB)
"Thus, you are to be holy to Me, for I the Lord am holy; and I have set you apart from the people to be Mine."

Pain

I STRUGGLED TO REMOVE my shoe. It was the slip-on type and usually just came right off when I used my other foot to hold it down and pulled my foot out. Standing in my closet, I reached down to tackle the issue with my hand.

Pain.

Excruciating pain somewhere in the area between my hip and back.

I was frozen in position.

Moments passed as I contemplated my next move. How long could I stay bent over?

When I could breathe again, I shuffled my way to the bench in the center of the closet. I yelled as I lowered myself. I have a high pain tolerance. When I say I yelled, I mean an instantaneous, loud cry of pain, surprising me.

From that moment on I moved in slow motion.

I don't like to take pills, but I began a regimen of Advil every four hours. I alternated between the heating pad and ice pack. The rest of my life came to a halt. Managing the pain was my focus.

I had already stripped my bed for the Saturday change of sheets. I stared at it. How in the world was I going to pull a fitted sheet over the mattress?

No position was comfortable. Standing after being seated produced the aforementioned yell, and sorry if I offend, but just going to the bathroom was a painful ordeal.

The next day was Sunday. There was no way I could shower, get dressed, drive, and sit in church.

As I write this, I am on day six. Just the fact that I can produce words from my brain is an indication that I am improved. I've taken no Advil today. Life is coming back into focus. And so are my thoughts about people I've heard say "my back went out" or "I'm having back trouble right now." My response was always to extend sympathy and prayer. I have a whole new understanding of what those words entail.

When I think back over the activities I have been unable to do this past week, my thoughts turn to the people who are permanently unable to do those things. My empathy for them has been taken to a whole new level.

As for me, my heart is now full of gratitude for the little things.

1 Peter 3:8 (NIV)
"Finally, all of you, be like-minded, be sympathetic, love one another, be compassionate and humble."

Penny Walks

MONEY WAS SCARCE WHEN I was a child, so entertainment had to be inexpensive. I spent a lot of time with an older sister who had two daughters. For pleasure, we took penny walks.

These were the rules. When you got to an intersection, you flipped a penny. If it was heads, you went right. If it was tails, you went left. And on the rare occasion it fell in a crack and stood on its edge, you went straight ahead.

Sometimes we went around the same block several times. Sometimes we traveled a long way from home and had to remember our way back.

But no two walks were ever the same.

Life is like that. Sometimes you go left. Sometimes you go right. Sometimes you go around the same block several times. But my question is this: Who is flipping your penny? Is God in charge of your walk?

Sometimes taking the walk is not your idea. I arrived at the intersection of "Divorce," although I didn't want that word in my vocabulary. For a time, I continued to go straight ahead because it was all I knew. Changing directions was so terrifying it seemed impossible.

Are you at an unexpected intersection? Who took you there? Do you tell yourself, "It's not my fault?" Is it your parents you blame? Or maybe your spouse? The list is endless. Friends. Church. Life. But the true question is this: What are you going to do about it?

I had never had "Intersection Training." I prayed for a neon sign to show up in my yard, displaying the answer. But as I cautiously emerged from my shell, I discovered the Bible was full of guidance about choices and what direction to go. I had to want to find the answers.

Maybe you need to make a hard right turn, right now, today. Are you willing to change directions? Perhaps your abundant life is down that road to the right. You don't want to miss out.

Remember, no two walks are alike. Even though someone else's choice for direction in their life may look appealing to you, this is *your* walk.

Deuteronomy 5:33 (NIV)
"Walk in obedience to all that the Lord your God has commanded you,
so that you may live and prosper and prolong your days ..."

A Special Sleepover

FINALLY, I SLEPT WITH my husband again. Let me explain. I hadn't slept with him since April 12th. And no, John hadn't been out of the country. The weekend of the 12th to 14th was his off-road motorcycle training. Learning to ride on the grapefruit size rocks was his undoing, landing with his hip on one of them.

Even though there were no broken bones, John was unable to lie in a bed. Thus, the big chair in the television room became his place for sleeping.

Not wanting to be clear across the house from him, I slept on the couch.

We thought it was a temporary arrangement, just a few days. But five days turned into ten, then twenty, then thirty. After forty days, John could finally sleep in the bed again.

I know there are married couples that sleep in separate beds. Sometimes it is for physical reasons, such as an injury, and other times it is a choice made to insure a good night's rest. For us, separate beds would be a punishment. Throughout the night, it has always been important to us to know that the other one is there.

For those forty days and nights, I thought about the couples for whom the separation is permanent. Perhaps their mate has been placed in a long-term care facility. For others, their loved one has passed on.

I never want to take the closeness John and I have for granted.

Postscript: A few days after I wrote this, John was diagnosed with cancer. I now sleep alone.

Song of Solomon 4:9 (NLT)
"You have captured my heart, my treasure, my bride. You hold it hostage with one glance of your eyes ..."

Apples of Gold

NOVEMBER 9, 2010, I posted my first blog: My First Baby Step:

Here we go! This is a new adventure for me, one I've looked forward to for a few years. My hope is that as you read the words I post, you will take the time to pause and let the meaning sink in.

If just one person leaves this website with a little different understanding about their life, with just a little bit more hope, a clearer direction, then my dream will have come true.

* * *

It is nine years since I wrote those words.

In 2010 I had no idea of the journey that lay before me. As my husband's illness progressed, my postings became sporadic. But I wanted to include my readers in my life—warts and all. So I shared my thoughts and emotions about death and dying, grief and grieving.

One year and five months after John's passing, my desire to write returned.

May my words be pleasant to read and perhaps touch your soul. We are all in this life together. I pray that my writings will be a "word fitly spoken," the right thing, said at the right time, in the right place, to the right person, in the right way, and for the right purpose.

Proverbs 25:11 (AMP)
"Like apples of gold in settings of silver is a word spoken at the right time."

Focus Point

OVER THE YEARS, I have had the pleasure of seeing some wonderful skaters perform, such as Scotty Hamilton, and Underhill and Martini. Their motions are so fluid and graceful as they glide across the ice.

But sometimes they spin like a top while staying in exactly the same spot.

I researched how they could spin like that and then skate off in a straight line. It seems they choose a focus point and keep looking at it each time they come around. The more centered they are, the less likely they are to feel dizzy. A good spin also requires the skater to have a strong core.

When John died, my life was in a spin, with me wobbling and moving from my starting spot. Paperwork, decisions, new pattern to my day, empty bed at night, sorting through my husband's clothes and property, all led to me spinning.

But just as the skater improves with practice, so did I. The first few days it was hard to focus and my starting spot kept moving.

But my focus point remained the same—Jesus.

Even though I continued to spin, my focus was certain, and my core strong. Each morning I turned to Him as my starting spot. I was not exactly skating off in a straight line, but the more I focused, the fewer wobbles.

2 Corinthians 4:16 (MSG)
"So we're not giving up. How could we! Even though on the outside it often looks like things are falling apart on us, on the inside, where God is making new life, not a day goes by without his unfolding grace."

The Purpose for Puzzles

AT THE BEGINNING OF each year, we are given the opportunity to put a new puzzle together. When the year starts, all we have is a pile of unknown before us. For some it looks daunting, while others see a big adventure.

Some puzzles are harder to put together than others.

Just as an actual puzzle goes together more quickly when you start by putting the edge in place, so it is in our lives. To successfully complete the puzzle of life we need the framework of prayer, Bible reading, Christian fellowship, and time alone with God. All of those components work together to form a boundary around us.

There's another thing about puzzles. They won't form a completed picture without work. We can pile the pieces on the table and look at them every day, but nothing will change. Life is just like that. It takes effort on our part to begin to put the pieces of our life in the proper place. Each piece of a puzzle has a specific purpose.

When John passed away, my family gathered and we worked on a puzzle as therapy. It was very hard, but I didn't put that puzzle together all by myself. I had lots of help. That is the only puzzle I have ever framed and hung on the wall. As I look at the completed puzzle, it is full of memories of the love of others. It's a constant reminder of the support I received to produce a beautiful picture.

We will have years that make sense. We will understand the world around us and know our place in it. And then comes the year when it's all a blur. Nothing seems right. We have no idea where we belong.

But no matter the difficulty of the puzzle, if we persevere and turn to God, we end up with the perfect picture He has in mind for each of us.

He's the Puzzle Master.

Jeremiah 17:9-10 (MSG)

"The heart is hopelessly dark and deceitful, a puzzle that no one can figure out. But I, God, search the heart and examine the mind. I get to the heart of the human. I get to the root of things. I treat them as they really are, not as they pretend to be."

Hamburger Gravy and Cottage Cheese

I SAT IN MY CHAIR, my Bible on the desk in front of me, spending time with God. As I read, I wondered if one of my older Bibles had some of my notes in the margin to help me understand this specific verse.

When I reached for the Bible on the shelf above the desk, it slipped in my hand and I almost dropped it. Pages fluttered and a piece of paper fell out.

Instantly I recognized the handwriting. Tentatively, I picked up the note, my breath on pause. Before I could read two words, tears streamed down my face.

> Thank you for loving me in so many practical ways,
> like hamburger gravy and cottage cheese.

I experienced a meltdown.

Sometimes I go for days without the intense sense of missing my beloved husband. At other times, it seems I just can't shake off the longing to see him again, touch his hand, and hear his voice. To connect.

God knew what I needed, so He provided it. Here it was, in John's handwriting, his expression of love for me.

In those moments, I felt so close to him, like he was right there in the room with me.

Who knew when he had placed that note in my Bible?

In this day of high tech, I fear we are losing the connection of the hand-written word. We can quickly send a text and then move on to the next thing in our busy day. What if we took the time to send an actual card, write a note or even a letter? We cannot be *that* busy to let those cherished connections fall by the wayside.

Somebody out there, somewhere, needs to read words composed by you, connecting. Words they can hold in their hands, stick in the corner of the mirror to read and re-read, or to place in the pages of a book as a keepsake.

1 Samuel 20:42 (MSG)
"Jonathan said, 'Go in peace! The two of us have vowed friendship in God's name, saying, "God will be the bond between me and you, and between my children and your children forever!"'"

Earthly or Eternal Perspective

I STOOD ON THE patio, the morning sun peeking through the trees. A gorgeous day was at hand.

We built such a lovely house, designed for our old age. All on one floor, wide halls and low maintenance. And John only got to enjoy it for three years. What a shame he can't delight in the home he put so much thought into.

Just that quickly I had another thought.

Duh. He's living in a mansion and isn't missing this house at all. I guess it's up to me to enjoy it, and so I will.

In life we are constantly given the opportunity to see our circumstances from an earthly perspective or from the eternal point of view.

What's going on in your life? Any chance you may need to change your perspective?

Colossians 3:2 (NIV)

"Set your mind on things above, not on earthly things."

Closure

Snowmageddon. That's what folks were calling it. Wave after wave of winter storms bringing blowing snow and slick roads. I had attended church on February 3rd. Then my church attendance came to a halt. It seemed each storm plowed through on the weekend. I honed my skills at reading radar and hurried to buy groceries on the one day between storms that allowed me to drive on the packed snowy streets.

Schools were closed. Churches were closed. Roads were closed.

On the 25th, I settled in to another day of blowing snow. A few more inches and we would break our record. It seemed like a good day to clean house. I dressed in sweats. After all, no one would be coming over, and I certainly wasn't going anywhere.

Taking a break between cleaning jobs, I picked up my iPad. For several months I had been contemplating buying a different car. The one I had was reliable and safe. It had only 39,000 miles on it, but there was one issue. It was exactly like the car John had driven before his death. A car that held many memories. Each time I walked into the garage and saw my car, it seemed like he should be home.

John had been gone almost four years at the time, yet I struggled with how to handle these spontaneous flashbacks. They were unsettling.

I clicked on the Archibald's website. That was where we purchased our cars. They were known for their high integrity and wonderful service. In fact, they were like family to me. I checked their inventory, and there it was. A car one year newer than mine—a different color and slightly different body design.

I pondered as I returned to my cleaning. Did I have a good enough reason to change cars?

Back on the iPad, I sent a message to my salesperson, a young man who was like a grandson to me. I asked him questions and he responded. How much difference in price? Was it one I would be comfortable in? Would it still be around when I could get out and come see it? Who would be shopping in this weather?

I didn't expect his response. "I'll come get you."

"Are you serious? I don't want to be out on these roads. Will you scare me? I don't want to slide."

"I'll drive really carefully. It will be OK."

I changed my clothes. I was going out after all.

He pulled into my driveway. I opened the garage door, and he helped me to the car, since the driveway was slick. He backed out, threading the car between the piled snow berms, and drove slowly down the street.

"This is a really nice car. I'm excited to see the one I'm thinking of buying."

"You're riding in it," he said with a grin.

"This one? Oh, my goodness. And now you are showing me it can go on snowy streets. You haven't slid one time."

At Archibald's, I was greeted with hugs. Then we got serious. After discussing the financial aspect, I decided it was within my means. I had explained my reason for wanting a different car and they all understood. John had been a friend, too.

Paperwork done, I was helped to my new car … into the passenger seat. I wasn't driving on that stuff.

Soon, in my garage, my old car had been replaced with the new one. As the old one was driven away, I took pictures. That was the scene I had watched, day after day, as John left for work. It seemed like John was leaving … again.

Once I got in the house, I sat on the couch. What had I just done? I didn't want to remove pieces of John from my life. But I also had a deep sense of relief. I needed to look forward, not backward. This was one more step in my grief journey.

I felt a sense of closure.

It took me a few days to share with anyone what I had done. I needed that time to process another phase in my widowhood. And I was eagerly awaiting the promised end of snow.

I really wanted to drive my new car.

Philippians 3:13b (NASB)

"… reaching forward to what lies ahead."

Eagles in a Storm

DID YOU KNOW THAT an eagle knows when a storm is approaching long before it breaks? The eagle will fly to some high spot and wait for the winds to come. When the storm hits, it sets its wings so that the wind will pick it up and lift it above the storm. While the storm rages below, the eagle is soaring above it.

The eagle does not escape the storm. It simply uses the storm to lift it higher. It rises on the winds that bring the storm.

When the storms of life come upon us, and all of us will experience them, we can rise above them by setting our minds and our belief toward God.

The storms do not have to overcome us. We can allow God's power to lift us above them. God enables us to ride the winds of the storm that bring sickness, tragedy, failure, and disappointment in our lives. We can soar above the storm.

Remember, it is not the burdens of life that weigh us down. It is how we handle them.

Isaiah 40:31 (MSG)
"Those who wait upon God get fresh strength. They spread their wings and soar like eagles."

Belief System

I AM NOT A morning person. Left to my own devices I would stay up until midnight and sleep in until nine. But life happens. Especially now that I have a neighbor who comes by and picks up Charlie to take him for a walk a little after seven each morning. So my plan is to be through at the gym by the time the dog walker arrives.

I set my alarm for 5:45. That's in the morning!

It's still dark outside. That's just wrong.

The other morning, I swung my feet off the side of the bed, searched for my house shoes, and turned on the lamp on the nightstand. All the activity roused the dog, so I let him out the back door to take care of his business. By the time he returned, I had donned my exercise clothes, complete with baseball cap, so as not to scare anyone, and was ready to leave.

I walked through the kitchen and happened to notice the time on the clock on the stove—12:24.

When did our electricity go off?

I looked up at the clock on the microwave. Same time. *What is going on?*

I pulled my iPhone from my pocket. It would tell me the truth, and it did—it was 12:24. What woke me?

I checked the alarm on my phone. It was still set for 5:45.

The confused dog watched me walk back in the bedroom, take off my shoes, and climb back into bed. When the alarm really did go off, I would already be dressed.

Sometimes life is just like that. We think something is an absolute. We go through the motions, based on our belief system. Then something a friend says makes us wonder about our belief. But we dismiss it. We find something unusual in a drawer. Again, our belief system kicks in and we choose to ignore that sign.

Eventually, the truth is discovered. The result of that discovery is up to us.

John 7:24 (MSG)

"Don't be nitpickers; use your head—and heart!—to discern what is right, to test what is authentically right."

Sort and Discard

SOME TIME AGO, I began a project that I planned to work on over the weekend. Boy was I wrong. Days later, I was still working on it.

I had 2,853 emails.

Now I know there is a way to simply delete them all. But I couldn't. Some were emailed receipts from purchases made. Others were pictures I wanted to keep. Still others were correspondence from when John was ill and then passed away.

You see, every email went all the way back to 2012. That's the year John was diagnosed with cancer. That's when email took a back seat to life.

Shedding a tear here and there, I worked through all the email—sorting, printing, and deleting. As I did, my mind turned to life.

There was a time in my life when I had to work on the project of removing negative input, untruths about God, and incorrect advice for my future. And that wasn't done in a few days. It took me two years.

What does your life inbox look like? Do you need to take the time to sort and discard?

2 Corinthians 5:17 (MSG)

"Now we look inside, and what we see is that anyone united with the Messiah gets a fresh start, is created new. The old life is gone; a new life burgeons!"

Meet Joy Bach

JOY BACH WAS MARRIED for 35 years to John, a wonderful man who has now graduated from this life's school.

Joy is a mom and grandma who loves to read, write, crochet, knit, travel, and spend time with family and friends. She finally retired at the end of 2017.

Her articles have appeared on the FaithWriters and Jewels of Encouragement websites, and in *Called* magazine. Her first book, *Life Moments With Joy*, was published on December 5, 2017, giving her a wonderful 75th birthday present.

Over the years, Joy has helped organize and lead singles' groups, taught classes for women, and been instrumental in starting a Celebrate Recovery group at her church.

Joy's newest endeavor is the creation of a group called Life After Loss. As a recent widow, she became aware of the need for support for women struggling to figure out their place in life after the loss of their spouse. The gathering meets once a week in her home where they discuss everything from how to pay bills to cooking for one. The camaraderie is uplifting and encouraging.

For more of Joy's articles, or to contact her, visit her website at:
www.joy-lifemoments.blogspot.com

CPSIA information can be obtained
at www.ICGtesting.com
Printed in the USA
JSHW021907030223
37135JS00005B/17